Tell Me What to Eat if I Have Acid Reflux

Tell Me What to Eat if I Have Acid Reflux

by

Elaine Magee, M.P.H., R.D.

New York

This edition published in 2009 by:

The Rosen Publishing Group, Inc.
29 E. 21st Street
New York, NY 10010

Design by Nelson Sá

Library of Congress Cataloging-in-Publication Data

Magee, Elaine.
Tell me what to eat if I have acid reflux / By Elaine Magee.
    p. cm.
"First published as Tell Me What to Eat if I Have Acid Reflux by New Page Books/Career Press."
Includes index.
ISBN-13: 978-1-4042-1840-6 (library binding)
1. Gastroesophageal reflux—Popular works. 2. Gastroesophageal reflux—Diet therapy. I. Title.
RC815.7.M34 2009
616.3'240654—dc22

                                                                    2008015311

Manufactured in the United States of America

Contents

Foreword

Eighteen percent of people worldwide experience acid reflux symptoms. While medical science has made significant advances in the treatment of gastroesophageal reflux disease (GERD), it remains a chronic and relapsing condition.

The fact is that GERD is often undiagnosed and unrecognized. Surprisingly, compared to the multitude afflicted, a small number actually seek medical advice. Self-medication is common, but temporary relief of symptoms can often be misleading. Complications of GERD can be masked by a symptomatic response to even the mildest over-the-counter medicines. It is known that those patients with long-standing reflux may actually have fewer symptoms with time, yet the disease may progress unbeknownst to the patient. The importance of making a specific diagnosis of GERD cannot be over-emphasized.

More recently, various organizations have launched educational campaigns making GERD better known. Recently publicized GERD cancer risks have piqued the curiosity of those having even the mildest forms of the problem.

As a practitioner, I have often felt short-handed with regard to providing my patients with detailed dietary and lifestyle advice. I have been impressed with a patient's desire to understand the process behind their affliction. The fact is that most physicians are consumed with the medical aspect of GERD and are not well equipped to offer patients new approaches to helpful dietary and lifestyle changes. It is those very things that are the cornerstone to the successful management of any medical problem, including acid reflux.

Tell Me What to Eat if I Have Acid Reflux offers a comprehensive review of the mechanisms behind reflux disease and explores its many manifestations. This work covers the medical and procedural aspects of GERD therapy and critically details them. Newer nonsurgical procedures for GERD are mentioned as well.

Most importantly, Elaine Magee's presentation of acid reflux disorders provides the reader with an easy understanding of GERD and provides a patient-oriented, realistic strategy to controlling the condition through better diet and living. Aside from sound advice about lifestyle, the variety of recipes is abounding and this book offers the reader a sense that they can be in control.

Elaine Magee has thoroughly researched the nutrition basis for the treatment of acid reflux disease and gives practical guidelines that will lead patients to a better quality of life. I would recommend this book to all my reflux patients as a perfect adjunct to their care.

— Anthony A. Starpoli, M.D.
Director of the GERD Unit,
St. Vincent's Hospital and
Medical Center, NY

(🍴) Introduction

A ll you have to do is say the words "acid reflux" and suddenly everyone you speak with either has it or knows several people who do. I think I've hit the magical age of acid reflux because now that I've hit the 40 mark, I hear more and more about people being diagnosed with it. Do I personally suffer from it? Not yet, but I do know plenty of good friends and family members who have been suffering from it. That's why I made sure to include a book on acid reflux in my *Tell Me What to Eat* medical nutrition series.

Acid reflux is a disease that should not be ignored or self-treated. But what concerns me is that nearly half of acid reflux sufferers do not know that what they have been experiencing is an actual disease.

In studies that measure emotional well-being, people with unresolved acid reflux often report worse scores than people with other chronic diseases such as diabetes, high blood pressure, peptic ulcer, or angina.

Here's the good news. Acid reflux is generally a treatable disease. Now, here's even better news. Most people with acid reflux have a mild form of the disease that can be controlled through lifestyle changes and medication.

If you think you may have acid reflux and you haven't already consulted a physician about it—that's the first step you need to take. The second step is working with your doctor to put together the best available treatment plan for you. No matter what medical course of action you and your doctor decide to take, the diet and lifestyle tips in this book will be a nice complement.

Don't suffer needlessly. Find out for sure if you have acid reflux, then get the help that you need to feel great again. Reading this book will certainly help put you on the right track.

Chapter 1

Everything You Ever Wanted to Ask Your Doctor About Acid Reflux

True, the majority of the book is devoted to the lifestyle and diet treatment options for acid reflux. Don't worry, we'll get to that. But first, you need to understand the who, what, where, why, and how of acid reflux. What is acid reflux? How do I spell relief from my symptoms? What are my medical options—from over-the-counter products to surgery—and what are their side effects and risks? Answering these questions is what this chapter is all about. It's about everything you ever wanted to ask your doctor about acid reflux—if you could ever have her undivided attention for about an hour or two.

Who has acid reflux?

If you have acid reflux, you are definitely not alone. More than 15 million Americans suffer from heartburn daily (a major symptom of acid reflux), with an additional 45 million having heartburn at least once a month. Do the math. That quickly adds up to around 10 percent of Americans having some degree of acid reflux disease. Globally, acid reflux affects about 7 percent of the population, including men, women, and children.

 What's going on inside my body with acid reflux?

When you have acid reflux, acid from the stomach flows backward up into the esophagus.

So the word "acid" comes from the stomach acid, and the word "reflux" comes from the "backward flow" (or refluxing) of this stomach acid into the lower esophagus. Sounds rather simple doesn't it? But this little backsplash of stomach acid can injure the lining of your esophagus and wreak havoc in your life. It can disturb sleep, make you very uncomfortable after meals, cause a great deal of pain and discomfort, and, when untreated, can lead to serious complications.

When the body is functioning normally, this backsplash of stomach acid should never even reach as

---

 ## The goals of acid reflux treatment are:

1. To bring the symptoms under control so you feel better.
2. To heal the esophagus of inflammation or injury.
3. To manage or prevent complications of acid reflux.
4. To keep acid reflux symptoms in remission so that daily life is unaffected or minimally affected by the reflux.

far up as the esophagus. You see, our bodies have a muscular valve called the lower esophageal sphincter connecting the lower end of the esophagus with the upper end of the stomach. Food is only supposed to flow downward from the esophagus into the stomach where the food proceeds to get digested. But in acid reflux disease, this valve relaxes too frequently and allows some stomach acid to flow backward up into the esophagus.

Q **Is there a cure for acid reflux?**
Acid reflux is a recurrent and chronic disease that does not resolve itself and go away. There isn't a cure, per se, for acid reflux. But long-term medical and lifestyle therapy is usually effective. It helps relieve symptoms in most people. Treatment options include life-style changes, medications, surgery, or a combination of the above.

Q **What is the most common symptom?**
Heartburn! 30 to 45 minutes after a heavy meal, heartburn hits. When excessive amounts of acid reflux into the lower esophagus, the biggest result is heartburn, which is described as a feeling of burning discomfort right behind the breastbone (or heart) area of the body, that moves up toward the neck

---

F.Y.I. Definitions

Definition of *Esophagus*:
The esophagus is the 10-inch-long tube linking the throat and the stomach.

Definition of *Esophagitis*:
Mild to moderate irritation of the esophagus.

and throat. The burning can last for several hours and is often the worst after meals. Having heartburn every now and then isn't necessarily acid reflux or a health "problem." But when heartburn is frequent (two or more times a week) or accompanied by other symptoms (food sticking in the throat, blood loss, or weight loss), that's when acid reflux becomes the diagnosis. Some people even taste the sour stomach acid in the back of the throat.

What are the other symptoms of acid reflux?
Besides heartburn, other common symptoms of acid reflux can include:

- A sensation of food coming back into the mouth accompanied by an acidic or sour taste.
- Hoarseness.
- Chronic cough.
- Chronic asthma.
- Belching.
- Bloating.

What can I do for just occasional heartburn?
For occasional heartburn, many people have found relief by using over-the-counter medicines and making some changes in their food habits and lifestyle, namely:

- Avoiding foods and beverages that may be contributing to heartburn (more on this in Chapter 2).
- Quitting smoking.
- Trimming off some extra pounds if you are overweight. (I know from personal experience— this is absolutely "easier said than done.") This is so important that Chapter 4 is entirely devoted to it.
- Eating your last meal or snack three hours or more before you go to sleep. That way you are hopefully going to sleep on a somewhat empty

stomach. The contents of the stomach should be small and therefore less likely to splash up into the esophagus when you lie down.

Is heartburn just the result of bad habits or does it have a physical cause?

You may be able to point your finger at bad eating habits for "occasional" heartburn. Habits like overeating at meals high in fat and over-indulging in alcohol and certain irritating food products like citrus juices, spicy tomato products, or chocolates, can cause heartburn—even in healthy individuals. But when you have more frequent heartburn and other symptoms and complications of acid reflux, there is more likely a physical cause.

F.Y.I. ## How do I know if my heartburn is serious?

Three things measure the severity of heartburn:

1. How long does a given episode of heartburn last?
2. How often does my heartburn occur?
3. How intense is my heartburn when it occurs?

It will help to know the answers to these questions when you visit your doctor or gastroenterologist.

Clues that it may be something serious:

- Having heartburn at least twice a week.
- Heartburn doesn't get better with antacids or over-the-counter medicine.
- Heartburn is associated with food sticking, weight loss, or a low blood count.

Q **What about pregnant women and heartburn?**
For many women, their first introduction to heartburn is their last few months of pregnancy. But there is a good explanation for this. The growing baby presses on the stomach, which can cause backward flow of stomach contents into the esophagus. The bad news is this type of heartburn is often resistant to dietary changes and even antacids. The good news is, once the baby is born, the problem with heartburn most often disappears.

Q **What is the key to relief of the symptoms?**
If the physical cause of many of the common symptoms of acid reflux is the stomach acid refluxing into the esophagus from the stomach, then suppressing that acid and keeping it from irritating esophageal tissue is the key in relieving the symptoms and letting the irritated tissue heal.

Q **When are symptoms the worst?**
Esophageal acid exposure in people with esophagitis is typically more frequent during

---

 F.Y.I. **Why stop smoking ?**

If you smoke, tobacco is making your acid reflux worse. Tobacco does three things to encourage acid reflux:

- Inhibits saliva—saliva helps coat and protect the esophagus.
- Stimulates stomach acid production.
- Relaxes the sphincter between the esophagus and the stomach, allowing stomach acid to splash up into and irritate the esophagus.

the day than at night, and especially after meals. Irritation and injury of esophageal tissue can take place directly after meals because that's when acid is released from the stomach and the esophageal sphincter can have a tendency to relax, allowing the stomach acid to splash into the esophagus.

For others, heartburn tends to rear its ugly head at bedtime. That's when all the foods and beverages we probably shouldn't have had so much of come back and haunt us. When you lie down to go to sleep, you shift the stomach from an up-and-down position to a sideways position, and suddenly the opening to the esophagus is level with the rest of the stomach and its contents.

 What are my treatment options?

Acid reflux is usually treated with a combination of diet and lifestyle changes, over-the-counter or prescription medications, and in some cases, surgery. Most doctors start with the least invasive, least expensive options, such as over-the-counter medicines and changing some troublesome lifestyle habits, and they work their way to more intensive treatments, such as prescription medications and surgery.

F.Y.I. **How often are you reaching for over-the-counter relief?**

If you are using an over-the-counter product more than twice a week, you should consult a doctor. The doctor can then confirm a specific diagnosis and develop a treatment plan with you, which might include the use of stronger prescription medicines if necessary.

The severity of acid reflux depends on:

- Lower esophageal sphincter dysfunction.
- The type and amount of fluid brought up from the stomach into the esophagus.
- The neutralizing effect of saliva.

Q
How is heartburn different from GERD/acid reflux?

Everyone experiences heartburn sometime in his life. But when the heartburn progresses from occasional heartburn to more than twice a week heartburn . . . or the heartburn is associated with any of the various complications (such as food sticking, weight loss, low blood count), your heartburn has most likely developed into acid reflux disease.

Q
Which drugs are best for acid reflux and how do they work?

The following drugs offer effective treatment to "some" or "most" people. Keep in mind though, that none of these current drugs used to treat acid reflux actually cures it. They help control symptoms and some also allow the esophagus to heal if there is tissue damage. Even when the drugs relieve symptoms

What is GERD?

GERD stands for gastroesophageal reflux disease. It is more commonly known as acid reflux disease.

F.Y.I. What is dyspepsia?

Up to half of acid reflux sufferers have dyspepsia—a medical term for "indigestion." Symptoms include heartburn, fullness in the stomach, and nausea after eating. These symptoms tend to increase during times of stress.

completely, the condition usually recurs within months after drugs are discontinued.

What do over-the-counter antacids and foaming agents (alginic acid) do?

Antacids are great for rapidly relieving heartburn symptoms. They work directly in the stomach to decrease the acidity of the reflux liquid irritating the esophagus. They also help neutralize the area inside the esophagus. When antacids and a foaming agent are combined, they produce a foam barrier in the stomach, which floats over the contents of the stomach, preventing acid from splashing up into the esophagus.

What they don't do

They do not heal esophagitis or prevent complications of acid reflux.

F.Y.I. For your information

Certain medications can actually aggravate acid reflux symptoms. That's why it is vitally important to tell your doctor about any and all medications you are taking.

What are the side effects of long-term use of antacids?

- Diarrhea from some antacids (Milk of Magnesia) and constipation from others (Amphogel, Alternagel). Aluminum and magnesium salts are used together in Mylanta and Maalox to help balance the side effects of diarrhea and constipation.
- Constipation can be caused by Calcium carbonate (Tums, Titralac, and Alka-2). These over-the-counter antacids are also obviously a source of calcium and in rare cases, can lead to too much calcium in the blood, leading to kidney failure.
- A change in the way the body breaks down, and uses, calcium.
- An increased risk of kidney stones.
- A build-up of magnesium in the body can be serious for patients with kidney disease.

If antacids are needed for more than three weeks, a doctor should be consulted.

Can they interact with other drugs I might be taking?

They can reduce the absorption of certain drugs (tetracycline, ciprofloxacin [Cipro], propanolol [Inderal], captopril [Capoten], and H2 blockers), so please let your doctor know if you are using antacids (even if you only use them every now and then). It will help to take the other drugs one hour before or three hours after you take the antacid.

H2 blockers—what do they do?

H2 blockers (also called H2 receptor antagonists), help inhibit acid secretion in the stomach

(Which helps reduce the stomach acid that tends to worsen symptoms).

They work in about 30 minutes and last up to eight hours.

There are over-the-counter H2 blockers and prescription H2 blockers. The over-the-counter version does not relieve symptoms as quickly as antacids, but they last longer. In other words, they may be slow to start, but once they get going, they help your acid reflux for a long time.

H2 blockers have been the traditional drug treatment in acid reflux because many of them can be an effective short-term therapy for resistant acid reflux symptoms. In most studies on H2 blockers, where the participants were taking these drugs twice a day, symptoms were eliminated in up to half of the people. In one particular study (participants took ranitidine, 150 mg, twice a day), people were healed of their esophagitis within six weeks (*Gastroenterology*, 1986; 91: 1198).

When taking these drugs keep three things in mind:

1. High doses are more effective than the more standard doses.
2. Taking them twice a day is more effective than taking them once a day.
3. H2 blockers are generally less expensive than proton pump inhibitors (see page 27 to find out more about proton pump inhibitors).

 F.Y.I. Do liquid antacids work better than tablets?

It is generally believed that liquid antacids work faster and are more potent than tablets, but evidence suggests that they all work equally well.

Over-the-counter version

A lower-dose, over-the-counter version of these drugs is available to help control "episodes" of heartburn, under the names cimetidine (100 mg), famotidine (10 mg), nizatidine (75 mg), and ranitidine (75 mg). They take longer to act than antacids (symptom relief may take 30 to 60 minutes), but they last longer.

You've probably seen these advertised on TV

Commercials abound for a couple of the drugs in this category. You know them by name—Tagamet HB, Pepcid AC, and Zantac 75.

For Tagamet (cimetidine), the prescribed dose is usually 300 mg, three times a day for four to six weeks and many people experience improvement after two to four weeks. Because antacids reduce the absorption of Tagamet, make sure you take your antacids an hour before or after Tagamet is taken. Some take the H2 blocker before eating and antacids after eating.

For Zantac (ranitidine HCl), the prescribed dose is usually 150 mg two times a day for four to six weeks depending on the response. For people whose symptoms mainly appear at night, a single dose of 300 mg taken at bedtime might do the trick.

•••

Warning—Even though these drugs are available without a prescription from your doctor, you should seek medical attention for persistent heartburn.

Side effects

These drugs, for the most part, have few side effects. Headache is the most common one cited. Other side effects reported are mild temporary diarrhea, dizziness, and rash. Liver and nerve disease exacerbate these side effects. Another concern is that long-term acid suppression with these drugs may cause cancerous changes in the stomach in people who also have untreated *H. pylori* infections (this also goes for long-term use of proton pump inhibitor drugs).

- Tagamet (cimetidine) interacts with a number of common medications (phenytoin, theophylline, and wafarin). Long-term use of excessive doses (more than 3 g a day) of cimtidine may cause impotence or breast enlargement (these problems reverse after the drug is discontinued).
- Zantac (ranitidine) interferes with very few drugs.
- Axid (famotidine and nizatidine), the latest H2 blocker, is nearly free of side effects or drug interactions.

F.Y.I. ## How do I know when my over-the-counter antacids or H2 blockers aren't enough?

Using over-the-counter antacids and H2 blockers to relieve heartburn, without seeing a doctor, may work well for occasional heartburn but they should not be used daily. If they are, they could be hiding a more severe disease and complications of acid reflux. When used in excess, these products can get expensive and may have significant side effects.

If you have heartburn more than twice a week or heartburn associated with food sticking, weight loss, or low blood count—you need to see your doctor immediately.

Promotility agents

These drugs are used for mild to moderate acid reflux symptoms and they are especially good at decreasing heartburn symptoms at night. They are often paired with H2 blockers to work together—they act in different ways to reduce symptoms. While prescription H2 blockers moderately suppress acid, promotility agents:

- Increase the strength of the lower esophageal sphincter muscle.
- Quicken emptying of the stomach contents.

Cisapride, bethanechol, and metoclopramide are the three promotility agents currently available.

Side effects

Metoclopramide can include side effects such as drowsiness, anxiety, agitation, and motor restlessness in up to 30 percent of patients.

Cisapride (Propulsid) should be avoided by people with certain disorders, including, but not limited to, almost any heart disease, kidney failure, apnea, emphysema, chronic bronchitis, advanced cancer, and conditions that increase the risk for electrolyte disorders (imbalances in potassium, magnesium, sodium, or calcium). And it should be used with caution in people with liver disorders. The Food and Drug Administration states that Propulsid should not be used by people taking antiallergy, antiangina, and antiarrhythmics (irregular heart rhythm drugs) medicines, and antibiotics, antidepressants, antifungals, antinausea, antipsychotics, or protease inhibitors (for HIV). The FDA also advises that Propulsid should not be prescribed to anyone with a history of irregular heartbeats, abnormal electrocardiogram, heart disease, kidney disease, lung disease, eating disorder, dehydration, persistent vomiting, or low levels of potassium, calcium, or magnesium.

Proton pump inhibitors

Proton pump inhibitors claim that they heal erosive esophagitis more rapidly than H2 blockers. They do this by decreasing the acidity of the stomach contents by inhibiting an enzyme necessary for acid secretion.

Doctors are using these more and more because they provide potent acid suppression—a quick way to help relieve symptoms and to let irritated tissues get a chance to heal. These drugs may help control meal-stimulated acid secretion, but acid reflux during sleep can still occur with patients who are taking these drugs.

The proton pump inhibitor drugs available by prescription are omeprazole (Prilosec) and lansoprazole (Prevacid) and they are only used when symptoms are severe and when there is damage to the esophagus lining.

What they do

These drugs maintain a stomach acid level of more than 4.0 for longer periods than promotility agent drugs. In the right doses, proton pump inhibitor medications are the most effective agents for healing esophagitis and preventing complications (something the other drugs aren't as good at doing). They also provide rapid relief of acid reflux symptoms.

Some studies have shown that the use of lansoprazole and omeprazole (two proton pump inhibitor drugs currently available in the United States) leads to symptom relief and healing of the esophagus in roughly 80 percent of the participants (*Gastroenterology*, 1997; 112: 1798).

What they don't do

They may have little or no effect on regurgitation or controlling asthmatic symptoms.

Are they safe?

Reported side effects of the drug omeprazole, although uncommon, are headache, diarrhea, abdominal pain, and nausea. Certain medications, whose absorption into the body depends on a certain stomach acid level, may not work as well when taking proton pump inhibitors as well as the promotility agents. They should not be used unless necessary by pregnant women or nursing mothers and they appear to be safe for children with severe acid reflux.

Q **Could other medicines you are taking be making your acid reflux worse?**

Medications you might be taking for other health problems can actually aggravate your acid reflux.

Check with your doctor to make sure you aren't taking the type of prescriptions that could be making your acid reflux worse.

Some cause the lower esophageal sphincter to relax. These are:

- Calcium channel blockers.
- Anti-cholinergics.
- Alpha-adrenergic agonists.
- Dopamine.
- Sedatives.
- Common pain relievers.

Some can weaken the peristaltic action of the esophagus and can slow stomach emptying. These are:

- Calcium channel blockers.
- Anti-cholinergics.

Some can cause damage to the esophagus lining:

- Alendronate (Fosamax, an anti-osteoporosis drug). Take this drug with 6–8 ounces of water— not juice or carbonated or mineral water—on an empty stomach in the morning and remain upright for 30 minutes afterward.

- Potassium and iron pills can be corrosive and cause ulcers in the esophagus.
- Antibiotics can make the mucous membrane more vulnerable to acids.

Nonsteroidal anti-inflammatory drugs (NSAID) are known for potentially causing ulcers in the stomach. But can they also harm the esophagus? One recent study found that elderly people who took these drugs and also had acid reflux were at higher risk for acid reflux complications (particularly strictures, abnormal narrowing of the esophagus, and Barrett's esophagus).

If you have been taking nonsteroidal anti-inflammatory drugs, you might be twice as likely to develop acid reflux disease, according to presenters at the annual meeting of the American College of Rheumatology. The results are from a study on people taking prescription NSAIDs for osteoarthritis. These drugs may contribute to acid reflux by relaxing the lower esophageal sphincter muscle, allowing the stomach contents to more easily find their way into the esophagus (*RN*, March 2000; vol. 63 i3: 96).

There are dozens of non-steroidal anti-inflammatory drugs, some of which are going to look very familiar:

- Aspirin.
- Ibuprofen (Motrin, Advil, Nuprin, Rufen).
- Naproxen (Aleve).
- Piroxicam (Feldene).
- Diflunisal (Dolobid).
- Indomethacin (Indocin).
- Flurbiprofen (Ansaid).
- Ketorolac (Toradol).
- Ketoprofen (Acron, Orudis KT).
- Diclofenac (Voltaren).

Note: If you have acid reflux, taking an "occasional" aspirin or other nonsteroidal anti-inflammatory drug will probably not harm you. But if you want to avoid them, Tylenol (acetaminophen) is a good alternative.

Is that an aspirin in your throat?

Sometimes acid reflux symptoms can appear simply because pills containing irritating chemicals become trapped in the esophagus and eventually dissolve. It can also happen with vitamin C supplements and antibiotics like tetracycline.

Which tests are used to evaluate acid reflux?

If your symptoms don't improve with prescription medications, your doctor may use one or more of the following tests to gather more information. An acid reflux exam often includes an endoscopy (described below). It takes about 15 to 30 minutes for the procedure.

- **Upper GI Series:** You are asked to swallow a liquid barium mixture and the radiologist uses a fluoroscope to watch the barium as it travels down your esophagus and into the stomach. X-rays are usually taken as needed. This test provides limited information about possible acid reflux but helps rule out other possible diagnoses, such as peptic ulcers.
- **Endoscopy:** After you have been sedated, a small, lighted, flexible tube is passed through the mouth and into the esophagus and stomach to look for abnormalities like inflammation or irritation of the lining of the esophagus. This is thought to be the best way to identify esophagitis and Barrett's esophagus. If the endoscopy finds anything suspicious, a small sample of the esophagus lining is often taken for further testing (biopsy).

- **Esophageal Monometry or Esophageal pH:**
  A small flexible tube is passed through the nose
  into the esophagus and stomach to measure
  pressures and function of the esophagus. The
  degree of acid that refluxes into the esophagus
  can also be measured over a 24-hour period.

When surgery is suggested

If medical treatment fails, surgery may be in order,
especially for young patients who want to avoid decades
of taking stomach medications. Side effects (usually
temporary) or complications associated with surgery occur
in 5–20 percent of patients (International Foundation for
Functional Gastrointestinal Disorders), the most common
being difficulty swallowing or impairment of the ability to
burp or vomit.

Anti-reflux surgery may not fix the problem forever,
either. It can break down, similar to hernia repairs in the
body. The recurrence rate is thought to be in the range of
10–30 percent over 20 years. In some people, even after
surgery, their reflux symptoms persist to the point of
needing to continue their medications anyway.

A new procedure called a laparoscopic fundoplication,
where the upper part of the stomach is wrapped around
the esophagus to increase the pressure on the esophageal
sphincter and keep acid in the stomach, is sometimes
performed. This procedure has a 10-year success rate of about
80–90 percent. People with an impaired lower esophageal
sphincter (the valve connecting the lower esophagus to the
upper stomach) are most likely to benefit from surgery.

New high-tech devices (recently cleared for marketing by the FDA)

There are two new endoscopic-based devices that the
companies claim provide an alternative to acid reflux

drugs and invasive surgery—the Stretta System, or "Curon" (Curon Medical Inc.), and the BESS, Bard Endoscopic Suturing System (C.R. Bard, Inc.). Both use an endoscope (a tube with a built-in camera) that is inserted through the throat to reach the valve at the end of the esophagus and the beginning of the stomach. Both devices try to tighten the valve, but this is where their similarities end.

The Stretta System uses a radiofrequency energy generator to heat the tissue, shrinking the valve opening, while the BESS device places small stitches (sutures) in the soft tissues of the esophagus and stomach—tightening the valve. This is an outpatient procedure and generally does not require general anesthesia. It isn't yet known exactly how long the valve tightening benefits last with either device.

What are the complications of acid reflux?
Only about 20 percent of patients seen by primary care doctors have a complicated form of acid reflux disease, such as erosive esophagitis, peptic stricture, or Barrett's esophagus (a premalignant condition where there is a change in the membrane cells).

Even if you currently have milder symptoms of acid reflux, complications could be waiting for you down the road—especially if your acid reflux isn't being treated.

 When your symptoms improve, your condition could actually be worse!

Believe it or not, when the esophagus is damaged, heartburn symptoms actually tend to improve. That's why if you have ever suffered from persistent heartburn, you may still need to see a doctor.

Overall, about 20 percent of patients with acid reflux go on to develop complications such as:

- Esophageal stricture (4–20 percent)—a narrowing or obstruction of the esophagus.
- Ulceration (2–7 percent).
- Hemorrhage or bleeding (more than 2 percent).
- Barrett's esophagus (10–15 percent)—a pre-cancer change in the lining of the esophagus.

(*Patient Care*, 2000; vol. 34 i17: 26)

If you have the following symptoms, serious damage may have already occurred and immediate medical attention is required:

- **Dysphasia:** Difficulty swallowing or a feeling that food is trapped behind the breastbone. (Almost half of acid reflux patients report having trouble swallowing.)
- **Bleeding:** Vomiting blood or having tarry, black bowel movements (this may occur if ulcers have developed in the esophagus).
- **Choking:** The sensation of acid refluxed into the windpipe causing shortness of breath, coughing, or hoarseness of the voice.
- Weight loss.

 How can you prevent complications from acid reflux?

- Don't ignore persistent symptoms of heartburn and reflux.
- See your doctor early. The physical cause of acid reflux can then be treated and the more serious complications of acid reflux can be avoided!

Q **What is the most serious complication of chronic acid reflux?**

Barrett's esophagus. The lining of the esophagus basically changes to resemble the lining of the intestine (due to chronic and constant exposure to stomach acid). This is actually the body's way of trying to protect the esophagus from acid by replacing its normal lining cells with cells similar to the intestinal lining. Although patients often say their heartburn has actually improved with Barrett's esophagus, it is a pre-cancerous condition carrying with it a 30-fold increased risk of developing esophageal cancer.

Q **Can acid reflux be making my asthma worse?**

Yes it can. Some researchers estimate that about half of asthmatic patients also have acid reflux. How do you know if acid reflux is making your asthma worse? Here are some clues:

1. Did your asthma appear for the first time as an adult?
2. Does your asthma seem to get worse after meals, lying down, or exercise?
3. Does your asthma occur mainly at night?

If you answered yes to the three clues above, here's some good news. Treatment of your acid reflux can make a difference in your asthma symptoms (it has in about 70 percent of patients). Some experts believe that the acid leaking from the lower esophagus stimulates the nerves running along the neck into the chest, causing bronchial constriction and difficulty breathing. It's also possible that a small amount of acid may be breathed in, consequently irritating the upper airway and triggering asthma symptoms.

What comes first, the chicken or the egg? It could be the other way around for some people. Could the asthma be giving you acid reflux? Experts are still figuring this out but wonder whether the coughing and sneezing with asthmatic attacks can cause changes in the chest and trigger reflux. It is also possible that certain asthmatic drugs (taken to dilate the airways) may relax the lower esophageal sphincter and contribute to acid reflux.

 F.Y.I.

Does having acid reflux increase your risk of cancer of the esophagus?

A recent study reported that people with acid reflux are at higher risk for a type of esophageal cancer (esophageal adenocarcinoma)—with or without developing Barrett's esophagus. A recent study (*New England Journal of Medicine*, March 18, 1999; vol. 340ill p825[7]) found that people with a history of acid reflux had over seven times the risk of esophageal adenocarcinoma and people with long-standing or severe acid reflux had a 43 times greater risk.

Some experts suspect that bile (not stomach acid) refluxing into the esophagus may be increasing the risk for cancerous changes. Bile is a digestive fluid made up of water, bile salts, lecithin, and cholesterol that is normally stored in the gallbladder and released into the small intestine to help digest and absorb food components. There is a surgical procedure available that is thought to be effective in suppressing both bile and acid reflux.

If you are asthmatic and you don't think your stomach acid is refluxing into your esophagus, you may want to think again. Researcher Susan Harading, with the Sleep/Wake Disorders Center at the University of Alabama, found that 62 percent of the asthmatic patients they studied who *did not* have acid reflux symptoms, actually showed physical signs of stomach acid in the upper portion of their esophagus over a 24-hour period.

Exercise-induced asthma, by the way, does not appear to be related to acid reflux.

If you are asthmatic and have reflux symptoms, strongly consider reflux therapy. If you don't have symptoms, but your asthma is hard to control, talk to your physician about esophageal pH testing to determine if you are having some acid reflux without symptoms.

 What ear, nose, and throat problems could be linked to acid reflux?

Do you have:

- A chronic cough?
- Sore throat?
- Laryngitis with hoarseness? (This can happen when stomach acid reaches the larynx or voice box.)

 More about asthma

Asthma is a chronic disease affecting more than 17 million Americans. When you have an asthma attack, cells within your lungs overproduce mucus, clogging the airways. The bronchial tubes swell and the muscles surrounding them tighten, causing the airways to narrow, and making it very hard to breathe.

- A tendency to clear your throat often?
- Growths on your vocal cords?

Acid reflux may be causing these problems. If these problems have not gotten better with standard treatments, ask you doctor whether they could be happening as a result of an underlying problem with acid reflux.

Q **Can acid reflux relapse after the esophagus has healed?**

Yes. Acid reflux tends to be chronic (of long duration) and relapsing. Eighty percent of people with healed esophagitis experience a relapse within eight weeks after the treatment has ended. And 75 percent of people who had negative endoscopy results after finishing successful short-term therapy with the medication omeprazole experience relapsing symptoms within six months. Those statistics will sober you up real quick. That's why preventing relapse is a top concern with acid reflux—it's right up there with relieving symptoms and healing esophagitis.

Q **What does hiatal hernia have to do with acid reflux?**

Hiatal hernia is when the upper part of the stomach moves up into the chest through a small opening in the diaphragm (the muscle separating the stomach from the chest).

What can cause hiatal hernia? Coughing, vomiting, straining, or sudden physical exertion can all cause increased pressure in the abdomen area, which can result in hiatal hernia. Being obese or pregnant can make hiatal hernia more likely. Many otherwise healthy people age 50 and over have a small hiatal hernia, but it can happen to people at any age.

Although hiatal hernias can impair the lower esophageal sphincter function, recent studies have failed to find that this directly causes acid reflux disease. Many people with hiatal hernia have neither reflux nor esophagitis. But the people who happen to have both acid reflux and hiatal hernia do tend to have the more severe acid reflux.

Q **Am I having chest pain from acid reflux or my heart?**

The early symptoms of a heart attack can be mistaken as heartburn—which is pretty scary. It is obviously extremely important to know whether acid reflux or a more serious heart condition, such as angina and heart attack, is causing your chest pain. Both heart attacks and acid reflux can each occur after a heavy meal has been eaten.

You can even have both at the same time! Some patients with coronary artery disease may develop anginal chest pain from their acid reflux. Some experts believe that the acid in the esophagus of such patients may activate nerves that temporarily impair blood flow to the heart.

It's always best to have your chest pain checked out immediately by a physician. But here are some hints that can help you along the way. These are more likely to be associated with acid reflux:

- Pain continues for hours.
- Retrosternal pain without lateral radiation.
- Pain that interrupts sleep, or is related to meals.
- Pain is relieved with antacid agents or H2 blockers.

Call 911 immediately if:

- You've never had heartburn before this, and you are experiencing chest pain and pressure.

- Antacids don't relieve the burning sensation in your chest within 10 to 15 minutes.
- Along with what you think is heartburn, you are also experiencing:
  - Shortness of breath.
  - Sweating.
  - Nausea.
  - Dizziness.
  - Fainting.
  - General weakness.
  - Pain radiating from your chest to your back, jaw, or arms.

These symptoms mean that you may be having a heart attack!

 How effective is lifestyle modification?
No matter how severe your acid reflux is, lifestyle modification is recommended because it is a low-cost and simple way to help improve symptoms and reduce the risk of relapse. In fact, 20 percent of people with mild to moderate acid reflux find that lifestyle changes improve their symptoms. But when people with acid reflux have esophagitis (inflammation of the esophagus), the most effective treatment is to reduce the acidity and the volume of potential reflux liquid by using acid-blocking medications.

 What types of lifestyle changes are we taking about?

If you smoke

Ask yourself whether your smoking is contributing to your acid reflux symptoms.

If you drink alcohol

Is it possible that your symptoms seem to get worse after you drink?

When you sleep

Don't lie down for three hours after eating, which means if you normally go to sleep at 10 P.M., the dinner hour should be no later than 6–7 P.M. This basically decreases the amount of stomach contents and stomach acid available to reflux when you lie down. If you like to snack at bedtime, don't. Anyone who snacks at bedtime is at high risk for acid reflux symptoms.

If you wear tight clothing

Try not to. Tight clothing squeezes the stomach and pushes stomach acid up into the esophagus.

If you are overweight

Try to trim down a little. Obesity could be contributing to your acid reflux because the extra weight being carried around your stomach can also put pressure on the stomach contents, which can push stomach acid up toward the esophagus.

When you eat

Avoid foods that lower the tone of the esophagus valve (fats and chocolate) and foods that may irritate the damaged lining of the esophagus (citrus juice, tomato juice, and pepper). For more on food-related recommendations, see Chapter 2.

If you eat heavy meals

You are at risk for an attack of heartburn, particularly if you follow that heavy meal with a quick siesta by lying on your back (or bending over from the waist).

Q **How do I sleep with acid reflux?**
For many people with acid reflux, nighttime is a living nightmare. A lot of this has to do with physically lying down and suddenly the stomach content has easier access to the opening of the esophagus. There are several things you can do to make acid reflux heartburn less likely when you sleep:

- Go to bed no earlier than four hours after having eaten your last meal or snack.
- Elevate the head of your bed about 6 inches by placing blocks under the legs at the head of the bed or an under-mattress foam wedge (to raise

F.Y.I. **The simplest way to raise the head of your bed**

You can make your own bed blocks by using a 4-x4-inch piece of wood and nailing two jar caps the right distance apart to hold the legs or casters at the upper end of the bed. If you don't use jar caps, you risk being jolted from your slumber when the upper end of the bed rolls off the 4x4.

the head about 6–10 inches). This slightly raises your esophagus compared to your stomach, so the stomach contents aren't as likely to splash up against the opening to your esophagus when you are lying down.

- The "right" side is wrong!

Doctors at Philadelphia's Graduate Hospital charted acid flow and sleep position in 10 people. While sleeping on their backs led to frequent but brief attacks, sleeping on their "right" sides caused the most pain and damage, leaving the left side as the proper side to sleep on because it caused the least acid flow of all. Although this study isn't the be-all end-all, try to sleep on your left side.

•••

Note: The most frequent symptoms of acid reflux are so common that they may not be associated with a disease. Self-diagnosis can lead to mistreatment. Consultation with a physician is essential to proper diagnosis and treatment of acid reflux.

Chapter 2

Everything You Ever Wanted to Know About Food and Acid Reflux

Y̲ou learn rather quickly by experience that when you eat or drink certain things in certain amounts, your acid reflux acts up. Wouldn't you like to know what those foods are right away, so you can be forewarned and perhaps forearmed (with medicines if need be)? The following is everything you need to know about how what you eat, how much you eat, and when you eat can influence your acid reflux.

A little warning: Some of the food suggestions are going to be easier to swallow than others (literally).

What are the foods I need to be careful of now that I have acid reflux?

Fifteen years ago, the standard anti-reflux diet called for restricting foods that seemed to bring on or aggravate acid reflux symptoms—spicy foods, acidic foods, fatty foods, as well as coffee, tea, and cola drinks. Two extra foods were also on the list of food "no no's" because they were thought to lower the esophageal sphincter pressure, which would encourage stomach acid to reflux into the esophagus. What are those two foods? Get ready, because I can guarantee you aren't going to like this . . . peppermint and chocolate.

So is this 15-year-old anti-reflux diet still the gold standard? Yes, with some modifications. These are the foods/drinks that act up acid reflux by either weakening the lower esophageal sphincter, increasing the acid content of the stomach, or bloating up the abdomen, causing pressure up toward the esophagus.

Foods that weaken the lower esophageal sphincter muscle encouraging acid reflux or heartburn and should be eaten in smaller portions or limited:

- Fried or fatty foods.
- Coffee (including decaffeinated coffee, which increases acid content in the stomach).
- Caffeinated tea and cola drinks (increase acid content in the stomach).
- Alcoholic beverages. (Although some studies have shown that small amounts of alcohol may actually protect the mucosal layer.)
- Chocolate.
- Peppermint and spearmint.
- Garlic.
- Onions.

Foods that increase the acid content in the stomach and should be limited or consumed in small portions:

- All caffeinated drinks (coffee, tea, soda with caffeine).
- Coffee (including decaf coffee).

Food that can irritate a damaged esophageal lining and should be limited or eaten in small portions:

- Citrus fruits and juices.
- Tomato products.
- Chili peppers.
- Pepper.

Foods that can bloat up the abdomen causing pressures that force acid to back up into the esophagus:

- All carbonated beverages.

I know the list above looks rather ominous. If you like Italian food, how can you get through a meal without a ton of garlic, onions, or tomato sauce! And if you are like most red-blooded Americans, how do you get through the morning without a cup of coffee?

How severe is your acid reflux and which foods/drinks tend to cause problems for you personally, in what amounts, and during what time of day are you most susceptible?

Why do I have heartburn every time I eat spicy foods (namely Mexican and Indian food)?

I don't know if you noticed, but spicy foods (other than chili peppers and pepper) aren't anywhere to be found in the lists above. That's because they don't actually cause heartburn. They just make you more aware of it—which definitely counts in my book. In other words, eating spicy food isn't going to increase the acid in your stomach or suddenly weaken your esophageal sphincter muscle, but when this happens and the stomach contents come in contact with the esophagus, the presence of the spices will help irritate the esophagus.

What do I do if I love spicy foods?

- Eat spicy foods in small portions.
- Avoid eating a large meal at the same time you have your small amount of spicy food (overeating in general, can exaggerate heartburn).
- Try not to wash your little spicy meal down with coffee (even decaf).
- Try not to take a nap or lie down for several hours after your little spicy meal.
- Chew some gum after the meal to help increase the flow of saliva.

What effect does alcohol have on acid reflux?

Some studies have shown that small amounts of alcohol may actually protect the mucosal layer. It is also known that a low dose of alcohol accelerates gastric emptying. This can be a good thing when you have acid reflux. The sooner your stomach empties its meal into the small intestine, the sooner your esophagus isn't being tormented by the stomach contents.

But that is where alcohol helping acid reflux ends. Alcohol relaxes the sphincter muscle (potentially encouraging acid reflux) and it can also irritate the mucous membrane of the esophagus as it is going down. In terms of digestion, you can get too much of a "good" thing, too. Whereas a low dose of alcohol can speed stomach emptying in the small intestine, high doses of alcohol slow stomach emptying (almost as if the stomach is confused and drunk), and even slow the movement of the bowel (*Am. J. Gastroenterology*, Dec. 2000; 95 [12]: 3374-82).

Which types of alcohol are we talking about? All types of alcohol are suspect, although some people mentioned a particular problem with red wine.

Q **If I switch to decaf coffee can I still have it?**
The roasted coffee beans that make coffee contain proteins that actually promote stomach acid secretion. Decaf coffee has these proteins just as much as regular coffee beans do. So, although switching to decaf may help with other health problems, it won't cure your acid reflux ills.

Sometimes it isn't the quality of food—it's the quantity

Even if you follow the rules and stay away from foods that tend to aggravate your acid reflux, you could very well find your symptoms are still fast and furious. This could be because you aren't looking at the quantity of food you are eating. The more you eat, the more of a load it will be for your stomach and the longer those contents will be churning away in your stomach. Eating small frequent meals through the day and eating light at night is a great way to eat for many health reasons (better for diabetes, obesity, etc.), so now you can add acid reflux to the list. There's a food step to freedom devoted just to this novel and healthful way of eating. You can read more about it, starting on page 52.

If your bedtime is 10 P.M., the last call for dinner should be 6 P.M.

Late night meals are a problem. Lying down shortly after you eat or drink is asking for trouble. The reason is purely physical. When you are standing or sitting up, your stomach is upright and the stomach contents have to work against gravity to splash up into your esophagus. But when you lie down or recline, the stomach contents automatically churn against the valve separating the upper stomach from the lower esophagus, because gravity is no longer holding it back.

To make sure your last meal has mostly left the stomach by the time you are ready to go to sleep, avoid eating or drinking for at least three or four hours before lying down. This means if bedtime is 10 P.M., the last call for dinner should be around 6 P.M. While we are at it, it is also a good idea not to exercise vigorously soon after eating, particularly activities involving bending or running—it also encourages refluxing.

 Are there any foods or habits that are heartburn "helpers"?

Saliva to the rescue!

When it comes to acid reflux, saliva is a "good thing." Saliva, which is alkaline, helps bathe the lower esophagus, providing a little protection from the refluxing stomach acid. What can you do to increase your saliva?

- Chew gum.
- Suck on antacids or lozenges.
- Eat sweet pickles.

 ## Can you walk and chew at the same time?

Chewing gum for one hour after a meal can reduce the time that stomach acid is in contact with the esophagus, according to a new study by the department of Veterans Affairs Medical Center in New Mexico (*Aliment Pharmacol. Ther.*, Feb. 2001; 15 [2]:151–5).

Eating slowly

Relax. Take your time eating your meals and snacks. You are less likely to eat a large amount of food at one sitting when you take your time and enjoy every bite. Eating meals that are smaller in size and calories help you avoid heartburn.

Eating small and frequently

Eating smaller, more frequent meals throughout the day and eating light at night is a great eating style for many health reasons, including acid reflux. For more on this, and holiday tips and recipes to help you avoid heartburn and follow the 10 Food Steps to Freedom, see Chapter 3.

Chapter 3

The 10 Food Steps to Freedom

oes the title "The 10 Food Steps to Freedom" mean that if I do these 10 things I will be totally free of acid reflux? I wish the answer was "yes," but unfortunately it's "no." The 10 Food Steps to Freedom means, if you put together the most important food- and lifestyle-related tips you have read so far in this book, you arrive at 10 food/lifestyle steps to bring you closer to freedom from acid reflux symptoms.

This reminds me of that joke that always begins, "Doctor, every time I do _____, I'm in pain and agony," to which the doctor replies, "then don't do _____." Just fill your own food in the blank—the one diet habit that sends you into heartburn hell. Something like, "Doctor, every time I eat greasy, deep fried food, I get heartburn something awful!" To which the doctor replies, "Then don't eat greasy, deep fried food!"

Everybody's acid reflux is different. Some people have milder symptoms and less esophageal damage, while others could have more severe symptoms or more advanced damage to their esophagus. Some people find that certain foods and drinks give them problems, while others say it's the amount of food and time of day that matters most. Some people battle heartburn during the day hours, while others suffer mainly at night.

The bottom line is that diet does not directly cause acid reflux. But acid reflux can be encouraged and aggravated by food and drink.

Food Step

Step 1: Eat frequent, small meals instead of less-frequent big meals

There are two ways to look at this food step. You can either look at it as eating smaller, more frequent meals, or you can look at it as avoiding eating big meals. Americans tend to do the opposite of this food step—we may skip a meal or two but when we eat, we tend to eat big. This is a tough habit to break. The key to eating small frequent meals for me is keeping this basic belief in check:

Eat when you are hungry and stop when you are comfortable.

In my experience, when we do this, we automatically end up eating smaller sized meals—which means we get hungry sooner—so we end up eating more often.

 F.Y.I. ## Keep your stomach comfortable, not full

A stomach full of food is more likely to splash up into the esophagus, so filling up your stomach is simply more likely to give you heartburn.

Eating more often, but smaller amounts at a time, is a good idea for every American, for a variety of sound health reasons, but it can be particularly helpful for people with acid reflux. Here's why:

- Smaller, lower-fat meals don't stay in the stomach as long as larger, higher-fat meals; they move more quickly to the intestines. And the shorter the time food is waiting around in the stomach, the shorter the time the stomach contents (including the stomach acid) are potentially splashing around, irritating the upper GI.

- Large meals fill up the stomach and are more likely to put pressure on the lower esophageal sphincter to open, allowing the contents of the full stomach to splash up into the esophagus. Picture an empty 2-liter soda bottle with 2 cups of liquid in it, screw on the top, and agitate the liquid. It is fairly difficult to get the liquid to splash around and hit the bottle cap isn't it? Now, fill that same 2-liter soda bottle with 6 cups of liquid. Suddenly hitting that bottle cap with some of the liquid is a lot easier now that the bottle is almost full. Your stomach acts much the same way.

What is it about large meals that encourages heartburn?

Is it the volume of food in the stomach? Is it the amount of calories? A recent study from Germany (*Aliment Pharmacol. Ther.*, Feb. 2001; 15[2]: 233–9) tried to answer those questions. They concluded that the amount of acid reflux induced by eating a meal, seemed to depend more on the volume (or space taken up) of food rather than the density of calories in the meal. In other words, these researchers are suggesting that if you ate enough of almost anything, even if it was low in calories, it could quite possibly encourage heartburn because of the amount you ate.

Other amazing benefits of "eating small"

If you don't want to eat small, frequent meals through the day to help your acid reflux, then do it for these other great reasons:

- Your brain and body require a constant supply of energy in the blood. Eating smaller, more frequent meals is more likely to keep your blood sugar and energy level stable, which can prevent headaches, irritability, food cravings, or overeating in susceptible people.
- The bigger the meal, the larger the number of calories eaten from carbohydrate, fat, and protein, and the higher the blood levels of those nutrients will be after the "large" meal. Large meals also zap you of your after-meal energy. If you've had a large meal, a nap is usually not far behind. But if you eat smaller meals you will feel more energetic throughout your day.
- It's physically more comfortable to eat smaller meals. You aren't weighed down by a large meal in your stomach. If you feel "light" on your feet, you will also be more likely to be physically active, too. And the more physically active you are, the more calories you will burn going about your day, which helps you stay trim and shed those extra pounds around the middle . . . which reduces your acid reflux symptoms!
- Eating smaller, more frequent meals is great for appetite control. The more stable blood sugars keep you from getting overly hungry, which can

lead to overeating or making high-sugar or high-fat food choices.

- One study observed that obesity was less common in people who ate more frequent meals. People who eat smaller, more frequent meals are less likely to overeat at any meal. Larger meals flood your bloodstream with fat, protein, and carbohydrate calories. Your body has to get rid of any extra calories. What does this have to do with being overweight? All extra calories can be converted to body fat for energy storage.

- This is still being investigated, but it is possible that this eating style may help lower serum cholesterol. It stands to reason that, by avoiding large meals, you also prevent quick rises of serum triglycerides that typically follow large, fatty meals.

- We burn more calories digesting, absorbing, and metabolizing food just by eating more often. The body burns calories when it digests and absorbs food. Every time we eat, the digestion process kicks in. If we eat six small meals instead of two large ones, we start the digestive process three times more often every single day—burning more calories. Calories burned by activating the metabolism can amount to about 5 to 10 percent of the total calories we eat in a day.

How frequent should the "smaller" meals be?

Experts have not yet determined the ideal eating pattern for people with acid reflux, but so far it seems that the closer together the meals are, the better the results. The longer the gap between a previous meal or snack and dinner, for example, the larger the dinner typically ends up being.

If you eat a small breakfast, have a mid-morning snack, a light lunch, then an afternoon snack, and a light dinner and maybe a nighttime snack, it adds up to six small meals for the day. Until researchers know more, the best advice I can give you is to space your meals according to your individual schedule, when you tend to get hungry.

Fight the urge to splurge at night

We burn 70 percent of our calories as fuel during the day, but when do many Americans eat the majority of their calories? During the evening hours. Eating small meals can break this habit. If you eat small meals throughout the day, eat when you're hungry and stop when you're "comfortable," it should be easier to avoid eating large dinners and evening desserts and snacks. Keep in mind that what you eat in the evening will be hitting your blood-stream pretty much around the time you are getting in your jammies. It isn't as though you are eating to fuel a marathon or anything.

Easier said than done

Our whole society is based on three meals a day—with dinner typically being the largest meal of the day. This is a hard habit to break. If you eat out often, it becomes particularly difficult not to eat a large meal. Restaurants tend to serve large meals and that's all there is to it. It requires extra diligence at restaurants to eat only half your meal and save the rest for later. If you are having spaghetti, you could eat the salad and half your entrée, then have the garlic bread and the rest of your spaghetti later or the next day. I'm not saying it isn't going to be difficult—but it can be done.

Food Step

Step 2: Lose some extra weight (if you are overweight), but not by fad dieting

There are those dreaded words again—"lose some extra weight." Don't you just hate it? Everyone always says it like it is so easy. Believe me, I know it's not.

Here's the thing though . . .

1. Being overweight often worsens acid reflux symptoms.
2. Many overweight people find relief from their acid reflux symptoms when they lose some weight.

The heartburn payoff may come sooner than you think, too. A recent study found that when overweight people with acid reflux participated in a healthy weight loss program, their reflux improved three weeks *before* their weight started to change. Instant gratification can be a very good thing!

But losing weight without falling for fad diets is such a complicated subject that we devoted Chapter 4 to it.

Food Step

Step 3: Avoid eating high-fat meals when possible to encourage weight loss (if appropriate) and to reduce acid reflux symptoms

Fried or fatty foods are thought to weaken the lower esophageal sphincter muscle, which encourages acid reflux, and that's why the recommendation to avoid fried or fatty foods appears in many food guidelines given to people with acid reflux. It has also been reported that relaxation of the esophageal muscle tends to occur after meals and that a fair amount of food fat in the small intestines appears to stimulate this reaction (*New England Journal of Medicine*, Sept. 8, 1994 vol. 331 #10 p656[5]).

But this food recommendation is under fire lately by some researchers who are questioning whether it is the volume of food or caloric density that is really causing problems.

Do high-fat foods really wreak havoc?

Whether people with acid reflux should continue to avoid those greasy, creamy, high-fat foods is being hotly debated around the globe. Some researchers say experience shows that many high-fat foods cause big problems for some people. Some researchers say it's the volume of the meal, not the fat. Others still say it's the density of calories that really does the harm.

Could it possibly be all of the above? Or are there other, more subtle ways that fatty foods encourage heartburn in some people? Such as the fact that the higher the fat of the meal, the longer it tends to stay in the stomach before moving on to the small intestine? Or is it that we tend to overdo our favorite greasy, high-fat foods, leading the meal toward a high volume of food or a high caloric density?

In one article (*Eur. J. Gastroenterol. Hepatol.*, 2000; 12; 12[12]: 1343–5), an Italian researcher stated that observations suggest that fatty meals, compared to balanced meals, do not promote acid reflux as long as the calorie load is the same. But a high-fat meal is more likely to contain the mother load of calories simply because every gram of fat is worth 9 calories compared to a gram of carbohydrate and protein, which are each worth 4 calories.

I've literally lightened hundreds of recipes over the past 15 years. I have modified the fat by using reduced-fat ingredients, cutting out some of the fat that isn't absolutely needed, or replacing a fatty ingredient with something much lower in fat and calories, and in every single case, there are always fewer calories after I cut the fat in half. Same dish, same amount of food in the serving, just half the fat and fewer calories.

If you want to go by the results of the recent study mentioned earlier, which concluded it was the volume and not as much the caloric density of the meal that influenced acid reflux, then what does that mean for fatty foods? I think of it this way. What types of foods do we tend to overeat? Do we overeat yogurt? Or steamed broccoli? Or grilled salmon? Last I checked, we tend to overeat foods like french fries, pizza, ribs, steak, chocolate chip cookies, or chocolate cake—all notorious high-fat foods.

One of the other big reasons the suggestion to limit portions of high-fat foods is boldly placed in this book's 10 Food Steps to Freedom is because people tend to lose weight and keep it off if they aren't eating a high-fat diet. This is an important point because one of the food steps to freedom is to lose excess weight (if overweight). So either way, it's probably a good idea to try choosing reduced-fat options when possible. For tips on eating less fat when eating "out" or eating "in" check out Chapters 6 and 7 and my latest cookbook, *The Recipe Doctor.*

Step 4: Foods and beverages that weaken the lower esophageal sphincter muscle should be eaten in very small portions or limited

Food Step

- Fried or fatty foods.
- Chocolate.

- Peppermint and spearmint.
- Garlic.
- Onions.

The following drinks are considered to be inciting agents (they encourage acid reflux) and they should be limited, particularly before bed.

- Coffee (including decaffeinated coffee, which increases the acid content in the stomach).
- Caffeinated tea and cola drinks (increase acid content in the stomach).
- Alcoholic beverages.

There is going to be a huge range of experiences with the above foods. I spoke with many acid reflux sufferers and they all had such different stories to tell. Some had no reaction or problem with garlic and onions, others said they literally can't touch them from dinner on or they suffer by nightfall. One man could have one cup of coffee first thing in the morning, but that was it. One women swore that drinking decaf herbal tea in the morning seemed to help her acid reflux.

What about alcohol? Does it matter what type of alcohol? Does it matter how much? Again, it depends. Some say red wine gives them the most grief. One man said one beer was his limit. My guess is anything with alcohol in it can weaken the sphincter muscle and encourage reflux if you have enough. The safest bet is to not have any alcohol at all.

The Chocolate Clause

I can't imagine a day going by without a little bite of chocolate. I usually have my daily "bite" right after lunch. Don't ask me why, that's just when my body tells me its time. A bite could be a "fun size" Snickers bar or a small handful of chocolate chips. It's not a lot—just enough. So I would have a big problem with the list above of foods to limit including my one favorite treat. So I asked around. One friend with acid reflux did OK with a small handful of M&M's but noticed discomfort anytime she had brownies. I asked the medical experts. Does it matter what type of chocolate? Does it matter how much chocolate? No one seemed to know—cocoa versus baker's chocolate, milk versus semi-sweet. How could they not know the answer to this very important question?

You will have to figure out for yourself what your chocolate clause is. Is a small handful fine, but more than that is off limits? Or is it that certain rich chocolate desserts (like brownies) mean trouble. And does it help if the chocolate dessert is lower in fat?

Food Step

Step 5: Foods that increase the acid content of the stomach should be consumed in small portions or limited

- Coffee (including decaffeinated coffee, which increases the acid content in the stomach).
- Caffeinated tea and cola drinks (increase acid content in the stomach).
- Calcium in milk. (It has been suggested that the calcium in milk increases stomach acid secretion.)

Reading this list is a little like déjà vu, because the same beverages were just listed in Step 4 as items that weaken the lower esophageal sphincter. Well, they also increase the acid content of the stomach. They are a double whammy when it comes to acid reflux. Some of you might find you can tolerate certain amounts of them at certain times of the day. Some people are going to be more sensitive during the day hours while others can tolerate a cup of coffee first thing in the morning but not late at night. You probably already know from experience when you are most likely to tolerate one little cup of coffee.

Food Step

Step 6: Foods that irritate a damaged esophageal lining should be limited (if your lining is damaged)

- Citrus fruits and citrus juices.
- Tomatoes and tomato products.
- Pepper.
- Chili pepper. (There is some research data that a phytochemical in chili pepper, capsaicin, may increase the sensitivity of the esophageal lining.)

Depending on the type of cuisine you favor, one or all of the above foods is going to be rather tough to temper. If you find you have discomfort with tomatoes and tomato products and you love Mexican and Italian foods, it's not going to be easy. If you find that chili pepper seems to bring on the heartburn and you enjoy eating Mexican and spicy Asian dishes, you aren't going to be happy either. You might be extremely sensitive and need to totally avoid the food, or you may find that a small amount, a virtual "taste" of it, is as far as you can go. You may even find you can have small amounts of the above foods as long as they are earlier in the day (say, lunchtime) rather than later.

Step 7: Foods that can bloat up the abdomen causing pressure that forces acid to back up into the esophagus should be limited

Food Step

All carbonated beverages are to blame. I would personally have a hard time never drinking a carbonated beverage again. I'm one of those Diet-Pepsi-a-day drinkers. And

 Crazy over capsaicin? The pleasure and pain principle

There's a fine line between pleasure and pain. And depending on your taste buds and preferences, you may actually crave irritating ingredients such as chili peppers. Capsaicin is the primary pungent and irritating ingredient in chili peppers and red peppers, which are widely used as spices around the globe. Capsaicin elicits burning pain by activating specific receptors on sensory nerve endings. Either you think it hurts so good or you think it's all bad. That's if you don't have acid reflux.

If you do suffer from heartburn, capsaicin can actually do a number on you, above and beyond its usual irritating or pleasurable "hot" effect in your mouth. It's possible that capsaicin increases the sensitivity of the esophagus lining, making it particularly painful when stomach acid refluxes up beyond the esophageal muscle sphincter. We'll know more in years to come, but in the meantime when it comes to chili peppers, pop them at your own risk!

man, am I ready for my Diet Pepsi by mid-afternoon! For many people, this food step is going to translate into limiting soda and carbonated beverages—not cutting them out completely. You may find that one soda in the afternoon goes down just fine. But a soda, after a fairly full meal, late into the evening may not.

Step 8: Have your heartburn helpers handy

The following foods and activities help by increasing saliva. Saliva is a basic (the opposite of acid), somewhat thick fluid that can help bathe your esophagus lining to provide a slight buffer to incoming stomach acid.

- Chewing gum (that isn't flavored with peppermint or spearmint).
- Sucking on antacids or lozenges.
- Drinking plain old tap water may help dilute the acid in your stomach and help remove acid that is coating the esophagus.
- Eating sweet pickles (has been suggested by some to help).

Step 9: Don't eat three to four hours before going to bed

Put another way, don't lie down up to four hours after eating. Back in Chapter 1, we talked about how when you lie down your body becomes horizontal instead of vertical, which means your stomach suddenly becomes horizontal, too. And if there is anything substantial in your stomach when you do lie down, it has a better chance of splashing up (refluxing) than if the stomach was right side up. When you are sitting upright, the stomach content has to work against gravity to splash up into the lower esophagus.

For more advice on how to sleep with acid reflux, check out the tips toward the end of Chapter 1.

The Bewitching Hour

The interesting thing is there are a significant number of acid reflux sufferers who actually have less of a problem at night, and actually have more trouble during the day hours. Most people, however, find that the bewitching hours are the ones that usually follow dinner.

Food Step

Step 10: Make other lifestyle changes that can help your heartburn

- Stop smoking.
- Elevate the head of the bed 6 inches.

The bottom line

It isn't an exact science. It all basically comes down to what, *when*, and how much. *What* you eat, *how much* of it you eat, and when you eat it can be helpful or hurtful for your particular acid reflux. The above 10 Food Steps to Freedom show you what tends to bother most or some people and helps explain to you physiologically how they encourage acid reflux. Beyond that, you have to write your own story about your own acid reflux. But hopefully this chapter gives you a running start!

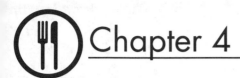 Chapter 4

Waiting to Lose Weight

W hy is there a whole chapter about losing weight in a book about acid reflux? Granted you can have acid reflux and be as thin as a supermodel. But the truth is that the majority of people suffering from acid reflux are overweight. And the excess baggage (so to speak), especially when it's around the mid-portion, can exacerbate the acid reflux.

Think about it—those 10 to 20 extra pounds around your belly are physically adding pressure to the stomach, which tends to push the stomach contents up toward the top of the stomach—generally not a good thing when you have acid reflux.

I'll tell you right now, I don't believe in fad dieting. It's simply one of the worst things you can do. First of all, the weight loss never lasts. Generally, there is only a 5 percent success rate when you look at maintained weight loss over a five-year period. And one-third gain it back by the one-year point. That means for every 100 people on these various diets, at best, only five people haven't gained the weight back five years down the line. Not only that, but anytime you embark in a quick weight-loss scheme, you are making it more difficult for your body to shed pounds in the future.

Each time you lose weight quickly, your body gets better and better at gaining and holding onto this extra weight the next time around. One of the reasons this is so is because when you lose weight quickly, you tend to lose muscle/protein mass. But when the pounds come back on, they tend to come back as body fat. This loss in muscle

---

 ## Quick weight loss — what are you really losing?

You know those books and magazine articles claiming you can "lose five pounds in five days"? You can only be losing mostly water if you lose five pounds in five days. Let me show you what you are really losing in those first few days.

Days 1–3 of a quick weight loss diet
- 75 percent of the weight loss is water.
- 20 percent of the weight loss is fat.
- 5 percent of the weight loss is protein.

Days 11–13
- 69 percent of the weight loss is fat.
- 19 percent of the weight loss is water.
- 12 percent of the weight loss is protein.

Days 21–24
- 85 percent of the weight loss is fat.
- 15 percent of the weight loss is protein.
- 0 percent of the weight loss is water.

decreases the amount of calories you burn just maintaining your basic body functions. The fewer calories you burn just maintaining your body function, the more likely you will have extra calories and put on extra body weight.

Just say "no" to dieting and dieting products

I fully realize that staying away from dieting is an upward battle in this country. Literally every single day you are being barraged by celebrities telling you how they stay thin and articles in magazines and new blockbuster books, each telling you how to lose weight fast—each advising you that this is truly "the answer." Don't believe it. Resist the urge and just walk on by. In case you still have a few questions though, here are the questions people keep asking me about fad diets.

 Do the high-protein, low-carbohydrate fad diets help you lose weight? Are there any risks?

Anytime a high-protein, low-carbohydrate eating plan is recommended it is not intended for long-term use. Carbohydrates, not protein, are the preferred fuel source for the body. When the body uses protein for energy, nitrogen must be removed first and all the extra nitrogen must be removed from the body (via urine) because too much circulating in the blood is toxic. This can overtax the kidneys. Anyone with impaired kidney function should not even attempt a high-protein diet.

Here's one weight loss fact you should always remember. Fat gets stored in the body when the calories we take in are higher than the calories we are burning—regardless of where those calories came from.

The long-term effects of high-protein fad diets have not been studied. It is true that many people will lose weight on these plans because they are mostly low-calorie plans and by limiting carbohydrate they are forcing the followers to limit portion size. The weight loss has more to do with the decrease in total calories and forced portion sizing and less to do with the fact that it is high in protein. But how healthy and permanent the weight loss is on this plan, remains to be proven. I have met several people who lost weight on one of these high-protein plans. None of them maintained the lost weight—each is back to where they started.

Q **Are high-protein diets more healthful than high-carbohydrate diets?**

No! But the high-carbohydrate diet is hopefully nicely balanced with some protein and some fat and features mostly complex carbohydrates (whole grains, vegetables, beans, and fruits) and not lots of sugar. Don't forget there are many important nutrients in grains, fruits, vegetables, beans (carbohydrate-rich foods), such as fiber, that are absent in those high-protein plans. High-protein diets are often high in saturated fat, too. Most can't even follow them for more than a few months because they are just too difficult to keep up. Bottom line is there is no evidence that individuals who lose weight on such diets maintain their weight loss.

Q **I keep hearing about carbohydrates—refined, complex, simple—what do I need to know?**

Don't be swayed by the carbohydrate-hating rhetoric out there. What is lost in the carbohydrate message is that there are different types of carbohydrates and you just can't lump sugar in the same nutritional camp as broccoli or whole-wheat bread—that's ridiculous. Certainly no one has evidence that we shouldn't be eating whole grains, beans, fruits, and vegetables. Now, lots of soda, fat-free, high-sugar cookies, and processed grains, that's another story. Here are some definitions to help you sift through the information.

Simple carbohydrates: Single sugar molecules or parts of sugar molecules bonded together. These single sugars are the building blocks for all carbohydrates. Naturally occurring sugars are glucose, fructose, or galactose. Table sugar is two sugars bonded together (sucrose and lactose). The sugar found in milk is also made of two sugars (glucose and galactose). Simple carbohydrates digest rapidly to form glucose molecules.

Complex carbohydrates: Long strands of sugar molecules linked together. They take longer to break down to glucose. Breads, pastas, grain-based foods, and starchy vegetables like potatoes and corn are excellent sources of complex carbohydrates.

Refined carbohydrates: Have had certain components of the plant removed, usually the germ and bran. Both simple and complex carbohydrates can be "refined." Table sugar is refined from raw sugar. White flour is refined from whole-wheat grain. Even fruit juice is refined if some of the pulp and fiber has been removed.

It just makes sense to emphasize the complex, unrefined carbohydrates. They contain the germ of the grain, which contains essential vitamins and helpful oils, and the bran, which contributes fiber and phytochemicals. Generally, the higher the fiber in a carbohydrate, the more "complex" the carbohydrate and the slower it converts from carbohydrate eaten to glucose in the blood, which helps most maintain consistent blood sugar levels at the very least.

What about the advertisements I see for foods and products that help you burn fat while you sleep?

To burn body fat your body has to be in a deficit situation where it requires more calories than it is taking in with food. This means exercise, building muscle, and eating less than your body requires. You know what they say— if it sounds too good to be true, it usually is. Anybody can tell you anything to help sell a product. Most quick and fast claims have no real science backing them up.

You should also avoid buying weight-loss products using "speed" substances such as ephedra, ma huang,

---

F.Y.I. So what can we do?

- **Stop dieting!** We know it doesn't work. We know it actually works against you. If you think back to your past experiences, you will know this to be true—if you are being honest with yourself.
- **Eat when you're hungry and stop when you are comfortable.** When you "diet" you force yourself not to listen to your natural hunger cues. When you do this, you also tend not to listen to your "comfortable" cues and overeat at times. In order to stop overeating, you need to stop dieting and start listening to when your body truly is comfortable.
- **Start exercising!** Exercising helps your body in so many ways. It is one of the fastest ways to increase your "calories out" side of the equation. (See page 89 for tips on how to start exercising—even if you're a couch potato.)

guarana, or high doses of caffeine. These may artificially increase your metabolic rate, but can be absolutely dangerous. These substances don't offer any long-term weight-loss advantages, and that's what really matters. Try to avoid the temptation of a quick fix. Trimming off extra pounds takes time. Concentrate on eating healthy and exercising; this benefits your body in many different ways—trimming off extra weight is just one of them.

No one can go on these fad diets for very long because you eventually get tired of it. And anytime you are "dieting" you are spending the bulk of your waking time and energy thinking about and following this new diet. Folks, that's not what life is supposed to be about. And eating should be about satisfying hunger, nourishing your body, and yes, even enjoying the meal.

Maintaining the joy of eating

Healthy food isn't going to do anyone any good if no one's eating it. Food should be enjoyed. With all this talk about what's good for our bodies, and what's not so good, that enjoyment part can sort of get lost in the nutritional shuffle. I don't want that to happen. Because if it doesn't taste good, chances are, you won't be able to stick to your new healthy dietary habits for very long.

There is something less obvious that can zap the joy right out of eating—counting. Counting calories, fat grams, or tabulating food group servings—take your pick. If you have to count anything having to do with your food, it can take the joy not only out of eating, but also out of living. Anytime you put yourself in a "counting" mode, day in and day out, you automatically snap into the "dieting" mentality, which often leaves you feeling defeated, deprived, and depressed.

Don't get me wrong, I don't mind periodic counting. That's when, every now and then, you check in to see how your average daily food intake compares to certain standards or recommendations. It can be useful as long as it is a checkpoint and not a daily regimen. There are people who, for their continued health, have to count certain nutrients (people with diabetes or renal disease). Believe me, one of their greatest challenges is maintaining the joy of eating.

Beauty is in the eye of the beholder

In some parts of the world and in other points in history, my curvy and round size-14 figure would be considered very desirable. It was only until the early 1900s that the Rubenesque women painted by Rafael and Renoir (around the mid- to late-1800s) were no longer considered the female "ideal." In their time, extra weight on women was a sign of being rich and healthy.

It was in the early 1900s that corsets and the age of the thin flapper dancer became popular. Then in the mid-1900s curves seemed to be coming back in with Marilyn Monroe, a gorgeous and curvy size 14, leading the charge. Unfortunately today, many women are embarrassed to be a size 14.

Then the 1960s ushered in the age of miniskirts, and bony women. I don't think we've shaken this yet, even after 30-plus years. Beauty contestants, models, and Hollywood actresses have never been thinner. To add confusion to the mix, obesity and eating disorders in this country have only been increasing. And yet these past 20 years we have, as a nation, fed billions of dollars into the dieting business. For what? It hasn't worked. We've never been more unhappy and more obese. Why do we keep pumping more dollars into fad diets. Why aren't we pumping iron instead? Why do we hate our bodies? Why aren't we celebrating our curves and focusing on health and fitness instead?

Call me an optimist, but I think the pendulum is finally swinging back a smidgen. Finally there are more "normal" sized women models, thanks to Emme and talk-show hosts (such as Rosie, whose "normal" size is 14-ish). And there are starting to be truly fashionable clothing stores and catalogues for women size 12–14 on up. It's like a breath of fresh air. I have recently noticed television specials lately on the new idea of "beauty" (which is probably really an "old" idea that's just coming back).

Just the other night I was watching a cable special on what men and women (past and present) are looking for in a mate. They interviewed men and women in parts of northeastern Africa and the men in this particular village said they were looking for a wife who was strong, had wide hips, and could have many children. I remember thinking, hey, they're describing a curvaceous and sturdy-framed person like myself.

You're not getting older, you're getting heavier

Marilyn Monroe aside, the sad truth is that as we age, body water, bone density, and muscle mass all tend to decrease while body fat increases. We can fight this by keeping our hydration and bone density as high as possible and by maintaining and building our muscle mass as we age. Sounds simple, doesn't it? If it were *really* simple, more of us would be doing it, wouldn't we? Hopefully the tips below will make it as easy as possible.

Trade in those fad diets for fitness

Most experts and chronic dieters can agree on one thing—dieting doesn't work. When tempted by new diets out there, remember this—quick weight loss tends to break down lean body tissue (muscles and organ tissue). Weight regain tends to put on body fat—exactly the opposite of what we want to happen. And each time you lose weight and gain it back, the more difficult it's going to be to lose that weight again. If you've lost weight and gained it back several times, then you know exactly what I'm talking about.

If we could all change our goal from losing weight to gaining health, we would all be better off. To gain health, we simply focus on eating healthy and getting regular exercise. To help us do this, it is essential we remember two things:

1. You don't have to be thin to be fit and healthy.
2. A healthy weight is the weight you maintain without too much trouble.

Get in a "health" mind-set

If you focus on losing pounds, you immediately put yourself in a dieting mind-set where you are more likely to fall into the weighing-yourself-daily failure trap. Change

 ## Obesity isn't attributed to a lack of willpower anymore

Obesity is now understood to result from a complex interaction of genetic, metabolic, behavioral, and environmental factors.

your focus to being and feeling healthy. I believe in eating and exercising for the health of it, and let the pounds fall where they may.

Don't give up just because you have the fat genes

We can't do anything about the genetic factors that influence obesity. On the other hand, we can't let our genes get in the way of our feeling good and being healthy. Your genes do enhance your susceptibility to gain weight in times of feast (versus famine), particularly when "feasting" with a high-fat diet. But if we eat a more healthful moderate-fat diet, with lots of plant foods, and we get active and physically fit, we are going to temper our genetic pull toward overweight.

We can also work on some of the other factors that influence obesity—such as the behavioral and psychological factors that influence our particular lives. We can look at our eating habits and what might be triggering us to overeat at times. If it looks like you have some issues with dieting, food, and body image, it might be a good idea to work with a psychologist or specially trained counselor to help you work through your particular past (so you can get on with your future). By the way, many people have long-standing issues with food, so please don't feel alone in this.

I know what it's like to have the fat gene on both sides of the family tree. My sisters and I have never been thin. But we were athletes through much of our youth and that helped us concentrate on what really mattered—health.

Take inventory of your eating habits

The one area you might need to look at more closely is changing the habits that might be leading you to excess weight. Do you have any unhealthy habits? Take the quiz below and find out:

The "What's Your Habit?" quiz

- Do you snack on sweets and chips more than fresh fruit and vegetables?
- Do you eat everything on your plate every time, thinking you would be wasting food if you didn't?
- Do you find yourself eating when you aren't really hungry because you are under stress, bored, angry, or upset? (Research indicates that using food to soothe feelings may be one big reason many people who lose weight gain it back.)
- Do you think you are being "bad" when you have your favorite foods? Do you think you must give them up in order to lose weight?
- Do you sometimes sit down for a small snack and end up eating a whole box of cookies, bag of chips, or small carton of ice cream?
- Do you sometimes let yourself get too hungry because you are trying to lose weight by not eating, even when you are hungry?
- Do you eat a lot of food late at night?

Now, trade the destructive habits above for the healthful habits below:

- Do you eat when you are hungry and stop when you are comfortable (not full)?

- Do you eat mostly plant foods, making sure you eat at least five servings of fruits and vegetables every day?
- Do you avoid alcohol?
- If there is a certain food you really want, and you are physically hungry, do you have it in a small but satisfying portion?
- Are you trying to eat more fiber-rich foods (fruits, vegetables, whole grains) and more balanced meals and snacks, including some protein and fat (mostly monounsaturated fat) because this generally makes meals more satisfying and staves off hunger longer?
- Do you eat light at night, knowing you will be more comfortable sleeping if you aren't full, waking up hungry and ready to start your day?
- Do you exercise regularly because you know it is important for your overall health?
- Do you avoid distractions—such as reading or watching television—when you eat? Do you try to eat slowly and savor the taste of food?
- Do you find other ways to comfort yourself when you are bored, stressed, angry, or upset? (Such as going for a walk, calling a friend, listening to some uplifting music, or taking a bubble bath.) Don't ignore your feelings—find healthier ways of dealing with them. It's easier said than done, but get professional counseling with this if you need it.
- Do you weigh yourself only when in doctors' offices because you know that the numbers on the scale really don't matter? What matters most is your overall health and how you feel.

Eat when you are hungry and stop when you are comfortable.

This is a big key to nourishing yourself. Don't forget this. It's important. But think about it—everything about dieting goes against this. Dieting tells you not to listen to your hunger. When you stop listening to your hunger, you open up a can of worms. Then it is more likely that you won't listen to your "I'm satisfied" or "I'm comfortable cues," and you might start overeating.

Know your food triggers

Many of us have developed certain triggers (environmental or emotional) that contribute to habits of overeating. Figuring out what these triggers are for you is a first, real important step toward squelching overeating. When your next food craving strikes (especially if you aren't physically hungry at the time), try to figure out what brought it on.

Sensory triggers:

Things you see, smell, or taste that make you want to eat (television commercials, walking past a particular restaurant).

- _____
- _____
- _____

Verbal triggers:

Things you hear that make you want to eat (someone talking about how great something tastes, someone telling you you've gained weight).

- _____
- _____
- _____

Emotional triggers:

Your psychological state or feelings that increase your desire to eat (being anxious, depressed, happy, bored).

- _____
- _____
- _____

Other triggers:

Anything else that triggers cravings for certain foods when you aren't physically hungry.

F.Y.I. **Binge Eating Disorder**

Binge eating disorder: eating larger amounts of food than most people would eat in a certain period of time (that is, two hours) with a sense of lack of control during these episodes.

Occurrence: It is estimated to occur in 20–50 percent of people who seek specialized obesity treatment.

Characteristics: Obese people with binge eating disorder tend to be heavier, report greater psychological distress, and are more likely to have experienced a psychiatric illness than obese people without binge eating disorder. They may have spent a great percentage of their lifetime on a diet and/or their weight may have fluctuated and cycled greatly over their lifetime.

- _____
- _____
- _____

Maximize your calorie burning

Should you eat fewer calories? You could, but that isn't very much fun. Your body needs more of various nutrients as you age anyway. If you eat less, you aren't likely to be getting more of these nutrients (such as calcium, vitamin D, antioxidants, vitamin B-12, zinc, etc.). And there are so many other health benefits to the suggestions below. You are truly better off burning more calories rather than eating a lot less. Here's how to burn more calories:

1. **Exercising.** Exercising, in general, helps increase the number of calories you burn in a day. Of course we know we burn the extra calories while we exercise, but some new evidence suggests we even burn extra calories after we exercise (possibly four to 12 hours after exercise). When you just begin to exercise regularly, you use mostly glucose (carbohydrate) as your main fuel during aerobic exercise. Once you get into a regular exercise program and your body becomes more fit, your body will start to burn more fat for the extra energy you need while you are exercising. Generally after exercising 20

F.Y.I. **Grazing is good!**

Eating small, frequent meals throughout the day and eating light at night is the best way to spread your calories out metabolically speaking (and weight-loss wise, too). For more on this, check out Food Step to Freedom in Chapter 3.

minutes, the new exerciser is probably primarily burning fat for fuel. Go for at least 20 minutes of valuable fat-burning time, then, you want to strive for those aerobic workouts that go for at least 40 minutes.

2. **Build muscle to burn more calories.** Muscle cells burn more calories at rest than fat cells do. How many calories are we talking about? About 70 percent of the calories you burn in a day are due to the metabolic activity of your lean body mass (muscle). If you want to build muscle tissue instead of fat tissue, exercise has to be part of your plan. For the best results use a combination of aerobic conditioning and strength training.

3. **Eat breakfast.** Your metabolism (the rate at which the body burns calories) may slow down to conserve fuel. One of the biggest gaps in eating is night time, when we sleep. If you are one of those people who isn't hungry right when you wake up, drink a small glass of juice or milk then pack some food to bring with you wherever you go. An hour or two later, when your hunger kicks in, you will be prepared.

4. **Eat small, frequent meals through the day, and eat light at night.** Each time you eat, you set your body's digestive process in motion. Each time you start it up, you burn calories. So the more frequently you eat, the more calories you burn just by digesting your food.

5. **Burn more calories digesting high-carbohydrate foods.** Your body uses more energy (burns more calories) to metabolize carbohydrates than it does to break down dietary fat. For example, if you eat 100 high-fat potato chip calories in excess of your calorie needs, about 97 of the 100 calories will probably end up as fat storage. But if you eat 100 higher carbohydrate calories as a baked potato,

for example, 77 calories will probably be deposited as fat (because your body burned 23 calories to digest, convert, and store those mostly carbohydrate calories).

How to maintain your muscle mass

Muscle mass and muscle strength also tend to decline as you age, because you start losing more and more muscle fibers and nerves that stimulate them. But you enhance your muscle mass through strength training and regular exercise. In terms of diet, you should make sure you are getting enough protein, but not too much. In this case, more is not better. The only true way to *build* muscle is to *use* muscle.

Start strength training, like yesterday!

Anyone can start boosting their muscle mass by doing appropriate strength-training exercises two to three times a week. You may have heard of these other terms for strength training: resistance training, weight training, and isotonics. Strength-training exercises usually involve activities that you repeat eight to 12 times in a row while standing or sitting in one place. The exercises pull a muscle (or set of muscles) to exhaustion. This encourages the muscle to grow and improve its tone. Strength training can be done two to three times a week for 30 to 40 minutes each session. Here are four great reasons to start strength training now!

1. Strength training builds muscle mass. Because muscle mass requires more calories to sustain itself than body fat, strength training helps raise your metabolic rate.

2. Strength training increases bone density so it also helps reduce the risk of osteoporosis.

3. The more muscle you have, the less insulin is required to get sugar from the blood to body tissues. Strength training helps reduce your risk of developing diabetes in your later years.

4. Strength training can ease the pain of osteoarthritis and may even ease the pain of rheumatoid arthritis.

So why are Americans getting heavier?

Those darn weight tables keep coming out. More diet books keep getting published. New drugs, herbal and otherwise, keep coming on the market. Jenny Craig, Weight

---

 I'm eating healthy and exercising, so why am I not losing weight?

If you are exercising regularly and strength training as well, you are probably adding muscle weight while decreasing some body fat. Remember, muscle weighs more than body fat. Your weight could very well stay the same even though you are building muscle and losing body fat. Keep in mind—you are healthier for it.

You could also take a look at portion sizes. It is possible, even if you are choosing healthful foods, that the portions may be too large for your caloric needs. If you keep this up, you won't see any actual lost "pounds." Or, if you eat out often, you may be eating more calories or fat grams than you realize.

Watchers, Slim-Fast, and other billion-dollar dieting giants have been waging war against weight gain for decades now! Never before have more reduced-fat and reduced-sugar foods been available. And yet, we are only getting heavier. What's going on? Getting back to the basics of weight control sheds some light on this rather sore subject.

One of the first questions related to weight control is: Do the "calories in" equal the "calories out"? That's because the net effect of excess calories (more than the body needs), even in the form of carbohydrates or protein, is going to increase the amount of fat put into storage (body fat). We know that most Americans haven't exactly been increasing their "calories out" side of the equation. Due to a combination of modern life factors (TV, long commutes, computers, etc.), Americans have become more sedentary.

What about the "calories in" portion? True, the average person ate less fat as a percentage of total calories during the National Center for Health Statistics survey period (from 36 to 34 percent)—but the amount of daily calories went up an average of 231 calories in 1990 compared to 1976. Now we're getting to the million-dollar question: Why would Americans suddenly increase their total daily calories at a time when the country has never been more obsessed with dieting and more concerned about healthy eating?

Ironically, some researchers think it is exactly this overemphasis on fat-free foods that has contributed to the rampant weight gain. Perhaps this wave has fed the belief that if a food has little or no fat, you can have as much as you want without gaining weight. Perhaps when people eat mediocre tasting fat-free foods, it leaves them feeling unsatisfied, so they eat more of the fat-free products or end up eating something else in the hopes of satisfying their hunger or food craving. Maybe since a large chunk of the American population is actively dieting at any one time, they continue to ride the unfortunate weight roller coaster of strict dieting and obsession, over and over again.

The dieting craze isn't helping

Experience shows that each time you lose weight you tend to gain it back and then some. And each time you do this you make it that much more difficult to lose the weight the next time you try. We have definitely been dieting (it's a billion-dollar-a-year industry) and we are definitely gaining it back and then some, so this could be one big reason why we are getting heavier.

It comes down to calories?

With all the new fat-free cookies and light products out there—how did this weight surplus happen? We are now in a culture where food is fast. Many of us eat out more than we eat in. Sweets are all around us. And soda is the number-one source of added sugars.

As a nation, we have become very aware of low-fat diets and because of that we have been eating more fat-free and low-fat products. But what we don't realize is, in many of these products, it's the sugar that is being substituted for the fat—with the calories staying pretty much the same. So we have really been trading fat for sugar. If the taste is only "alright" or if we are in the mind-set that we can eat more because it's "fat-free," then we are actually eating more (and getting more calories) with some of the products.

Surveys have shown that we are eating fewer percent calories from fat than 15–20 years ago, but they are also showing that we are eating *more calories* and more added sugars. We are actually eating 300 more calories a day when you compare data between 1975 and 1995. Not good, especially when you factor in that we are less active (burning fewer calories) than we were back then.

Reducing dietary fat alone, without reducing calories, is not going to encourage weight loss. But if you reduce food fat along with reducing carbohydrates—calories will decrease and weight loss will be possible.

If we ate more fruits, vegetables, beans, and whole grains, we would be eating fewer calories per a certain volume of food compared to a higher meats and sweets type of food fare.

If we are eating less fat and we are only getting fatter, then should we eat more fat to lose weight?

First of all, that's not really true, we aren't really eating less fat. Although Americans consume fewer "percent calories from fat" the actual number of grams that we take in has actually increased from 81 to 83 grams a day. How can the percent calories from fat decrease if we are eating 2 grams more fat per day? Because we have been eating *more calories* per day. So what's the big deal between eating 81 and 83 grams of fat a day, you say?

This computes out to an extra:
- 18 extra fat calories a day.
- 126 extra fat calories a week.
- 540 extra fat calories a month.
- 6,500 extra fat calories a year.

An important piece of the puzzle—exercise

Working on our "calories out" side of the weight-loss equation is a must—along with our food choices and amounts (the "calories in" portion of the equation). There are a few ways to increase our calories out—or the amount of calories we burn or use up as fuel. Exercise plays an important role in the first two ways.

1. We can move our body more and exercise, which requires calories.
2. We can increase our muscle in our body, which increases our metabolic rate.
3. We can adjust our food choices to maximize calorie burning due to digestion.

How to start exercising— even if you are a couch potato

The bottom line is that physical activity can make the difference between losing weight and not losing

---

 ## Read this before you start exercising if you have acid reflux

Don't exercise, particularly by doing activities that involve bending or running, soon after eating. When you bend over or jump around with a somewhat full stomach, your stomach is bending and jumping too— encouraging stomach acid to reflux into the lower esophagus. Find out when your body is most comfortable exercising. For me it's either after work but before dinner or it's several hours after dinner but before bed (I like to ride my stationary bike while I watch some of my favorite evening TV shows). For others it might be first thing in the morning.

weight. And if that isn't enough to get you off the couch, regular exercise has been shown to lower high triglyceride levels in the blood and lower high blood pressure after only 10 weeks. The risk of heart attack also decreases with regular exercise.

Exercise has psychological benefits, too—it simply makes you feel better. It encourages better sleep, gives you more energy throughout the day, helps you feel better about your body even if pounds haven't been lost, and it also helps reduce depression and stress.

Of the above benefits though, helping us trim extra fat around the middle and helping reduce stress are the two benefits most likely to help your acid reflux symptoms.

I can go over and over all the various benefits of exercise and I can even hold your hand and follow you around for a month helping you get in the habit of exercising. But sooner or later it is all going to come back to one person—you. Ultimately you have to take responsibility for your exercise habits.

The first step is to commit to trying "exercise" for one month, remembering to start slowly. At the end of one month you should hopefully have experienced many of the psychological and physiological benefits of exercise and you will be adequately "hooked." So let's look at how to get started:

- Visit your doctor and make sure you can proceed with your plans to start exercising.
- Don't make it a big weight-loss contest—focus on health and gaining better control of your blood sugar.
- It has to be fun or you are definitely not going to stick with it.
- Next, find out what your exercise preferences and needs are and try to consider them when making your exercise plans.
- Do you like exercising indoors or outdoors?

- Do you like to exercise alone, with a partner, or with a group?
- Do you like the gym atmosphere?
- What time of day would you be most likely to stick to exercising?
- Do you have any physical limitations that need to be considered? If you have joint limitations, for example, water aerobics or swimming can actually be a great starting place.
- What do you like to do? Even if your answer is watching television or talking, they can be worked into your exercise program. If you like to talk, walking with a partner might be the ticket. If you like to watch television, then home exercise equipment that you can use in the comfort of your family room or bedroom might be your most practical option.

Every little bit helps

Even if you can't imagine exercising 30 minutes or more in one sitting, split it up into three 10-minute mini-workouts. Ten minutes of activity here and there does add up to health benefits for your body. Any way that you can increase your activity throughout your day will help your cause.

Strength training gives you more than strength

The more muscle you have, the more calories and fat you burn—even sitting at the computer. That's because the more muscle you have, the higher your metabolic rate (the amount of calories your body burns just maintaining itself). So how do we make more muscle? The only way to build muscle is to use muscle. A great way to work your muscles directly is by strength training or resistance training.

But before you start buying dumbbells, keep these things in mind:

- Consult your doctor and a strength-training instructor. The exercises must be done properly to prevent injury and to build muscle strength.

- Do exercises in front of a mirror at first, to be sure your form matches the instructor (especially if you are working from a strength-training video).

- Start off strengthening the largest muscles in your body (muscles in the legs, back, and chest). You'll get the biggest metabolic bang for your buck this way.

- Start with whatever weight you feel comfortable lifting, but generally, you want to lift a weight that's heavy enough to make you feel fatigued after nine or so repititions. Starting out with overly heavy weights can lead to injuries.

- According to the American College of Sports Medicine, a single set of six to 12 repetitions is a great place to start. For beginners, single sets are just as effective as multiple sets.

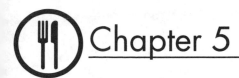

Chapter 5

How to Have a Heartburn-Free Holiday

A sk any heartburn sufferer if there is a time of year when they tend to be particularly uncomfortable and most will tell you "the holiday season." For many, it's a given. If it's the holidays, then get ready for heartburn.

That's because this is the no-holds-barred time of year when we break any food rules we may have had during the year. We are celebrating the season and with all the festivities, overindulgence is sure to follow—along with the worst acid reflux you've ever known. This is the last thing you want or need during this high stakes time of year. Even the stress of the holidays can add to the acid reflux risk.

Think about how we eat during the holiday season. We do exactly the opposite of the 10 Food Steps to Freedom:

- We indulge in high-fat foods and foods we don't normally have.
- We literally "feast" at our holiday feasts— eating large amounts of food at one sitting.
- We often eat these extra-large meals in the evening, just a few hours before we turn in for the night.
- And I would go so far as to say that tight clothing is a given, too. (Tight clothing puts pressure on the stomach, which can help push stomach contents up into the esophagus.)

So, to help you have a heartburn-free holiday, I've put together some quick tips and some feast and party recipes to shed some "light" on holiday eating. Of course if you are going to use the holiday recipes, there's a little catch. (Isn't there always?) You, or someone you love, will have to cook at least part of the holiday meal. But don't panic, these recipes are not only light in fat and calories, but they're light on time and effort, too. This chapter hopefully covers the bases with recipes for everything from appetizers to favorite holiday side dishes to delectable desserts.

So what can I do to avoid heartburn during the holidays?

Stuffing ourselves with food we eat once a year, eating lots of rich, fatty food . . . that's what inevitably happens during the holidays. All of this is loads of fun until the heartburn hits with a vengeance. Here are 10 tips to get you through the holidays—hopefully heartburn free.

10 tips toward
a heartburn-free holiday

1. Don't lie down on a full stomach. Stop eating and drinking around 7 P.M., then turn in around 11 (four hours later), once the stomach contents have mostly left the stomach.

2. Try to avoid eating large amounts of the foods that tend to relax the lower esophageal sphincter (onions, chocolate, and foods high in fat).

3. Another reason to avoid eating a lot of high-fat foods is that the higher the fat in your meal, the longer it will linger in your stomach before going on to the small intestine, and the longer the stomach will be full of potentially troubling foodstuffs.

4. Avoid eating foods that can directly irritate an already inflamed esophagus (citrus juices, tomatoes).

5. Avoid drinking beverages that can directly irritate an already inflamed esophagus (soft drinks, coffee, and tea). So if you avoid soft drinks, coffee, and tea, what's left? Basically non-citrus juices, tomato juices, milk, and water. If you decide to imbibe in soft drinks, coffee, or tea, at least try and keep it to a minimum—keep it to one precious cup.

6. Avoid bending over, doing any heavy lifting, or running after a big meal. This can increase pressure in the stomach and can aggravate heartburn.

7. Relax during the holidays—if you can. Emotional stress and anxiety can aggravate heartburn.

8. Keep portions to a minimum. As hard and impossible as this sounds, try not to eat those "eat till you explode" large meals. Passing up

"seconds" will usually do the trick. I know everything tastes so good, so bring some leftovers home and enjoy the whole dinner again—tomorrow.

9. Make better choices. When confronted with the typical party/holiday nibbles, know which ones are less likely to give you trouble (which is probably the ones lower in fat).

10. Offer to bring food to the party or holiday meal that you know you can eat without problems. You can bring lower fat (or lower spice) renditions of favorite party foods, if your system tends to have trouble with this. Make a lower fat dip using fat-free or light sour cream. Make a lower fat spread (such as crab or salmon) by using light cream cheese and cut out any added butter completely. And don't forget to eat slowly and enjoy it!

Thanksgiving menu ideas

What's Thanksgiving dinner without turkey and all the trimmings? Without heaps of fluffy, white potatoes doused in thick gravy, the scoops of moist and savory stuffing, sweet potatoes baked in a glaze of butter and brown sugar, followed by a hefty wedge of pumpkin pie?

No one here is trying to take away the traditional flavors of Thanksgiving, believe me. We have ways of making mashed potatoes, gravy, stuffing, sweet potatoes, and pie a few pounds lighter (in fat) without compromising taste and integrity. I've taken the liberty of developing lighter versions of some traditional Thanksgiving fixings. Here are the fat grams and calorie savings for a reduced-fat version (compared with the traditional dinner) of 4 ounces of roasted turkey breast, a serving of sausage stuffing, mashed potatoes and gravy, and a slice of pumpkin pie:

- Calories: 1,210733477
- Fat grams: 6219.542.5

F.Y.I. ## 6 easy ways to reduce the richness in holiday foods

- Most pumpkin pie recipes call for at least 1 cup of cream or evaporated whole milk and 2 eggs. Using evaporated skim milk and 3 egg whites will cut off about 300 calories and 30–38 grams of fat.

- Buying brown-and-serve rolls instead of the higher-fat crescent-type rolls will cut off about 1,100 extra calories and about 100 grams of fat per dozen.

- Using light cream cheese instead of regular cream cheese in your holiday dips, spreads, and cheesecakes will cut off about 16 grams of fat per cup of cream cheese.

- Using a great tasting fat-free sour cream (I recommend "Naturally Yours" brand in the black-and-white cowhide container) for your dips and spreads and potato dishes will cut off about 320 calories and about 35 grams of fat per cup of sour cream.

- Using reduced-fat cheese in your cheese logs, appetizers, and side dishes will cut off 36 grams of fat and 320 calories for every 8 oz.

- Making your dips and side dishes and appetizers with a mixture of real mayonnaise and fat-free sour cream. (For every cup of mayo blend 1/4 cup mayo with 3/4 cup of fat-free sour cream.) This mix will cut off over 1,000 calories and 132 grams of fat per cup of mayonnaise.

Lightened Thanksgiving recipes

 Pumpkin Custard Pie

Makes 12 servings.

- 1/3 cup sugar.
- 1/3 cup brown sugar.
- 3/4 tsp. ground cinnamon.
- 1/2 tsp. ground nutmeg.
- Pinch of ground cloves.
- 1 1/2 cups canned pumpkin.
- 1 tsp. vanilla extract.
- 1 1/4 cups evaporated skim milk.
- 1 tbs. freshly grated orange peel.
- 3 egg whites, lightly beaten.
- 1/4 cup orange juice.
- Single pie crust.

1. Preheat oven to 425 degrees.
2. In a mixing bowl, combine sugars, cinnamon, nutmeg, and cloves. Stir in pumpkin. Add vanilla, evaporated milk, orange peel, and egg whites. Beat with an electric mixer until smooth. Fold in orange juice.
3. Pour into a 9-inch unbaked pie crust and bake for 10 minutes. Reduce heat to 325 degrees and bake for 45 minutes or until knife inserted in the filling comes out clean. Let cool and refrigerate until served. Serve with light Cool Whip or a dollop of whipping cream if desired.

Per serving: 180 calories, 4.5 g protein, 27 g carbohydrate, 6 g fat, 1 mg cholesterol, 1 gram fiber, 145 mg sodium. Calories from fat: 30 percent.

Quick Sherry Cake (with Hot Buttered Sherry Glaze)

Makes 12 servings.

- Canola cooking spray.
- 1 box Duncan Hines moist deluxe butter recipe golden cake mix (or similar).
- 1 package (4 serving size) instant vanilla pudding mix.
- 1/2 tsp. ground nutmeg.
- 1 large egg.
- 1/2 cup egg substitute.
- 3/4 cup cream sherry.
- 2 tbs. canola oil.
- 1/2 cup and 2 tbs. fat-free sour cream (light can be substituted).

Glaze:

- 1/2 cup powdered sugar.
- 1 tbs. cream sherry.
- 1 tbs. melted butter.

1. Preheat oven to 375 degrees (if using a metal or glass pan) or 350 degrees (if using a dark or coated pan—and add 3–5 minutes to baking time). Coat sides and bottom of a bunt or tube pan with canola cooking spray.

2. Combine cake mix, pudding mix, nutmeg, egg, egg substitute, sherry, oil, and sour cream in large mixing bowl. Blend at low speed until moistened (about 30 seconds). Scrape sides of bowl.

3. Beat at medium speed for exactly 3 minutes. Pour batter in prepared pan and bake immediately (place

in center of oven). Bake for about 33–35 minutes. Cake is done when toothpick inserted in center of cake comes out clean. Cool in pan on rack for 15 minutes.

4. While cake is cooling, blend glaze ingredients in 1 cup measure. Poke holes in top of cake with fork. Drizzle glaze over the top of cake and enjoy!

Per serving: 313 calories, 6 g protein, 50 g carbohydrate, 7.5 g fat, 1.5 g saturated fat, 20 mg cholesterol, .6 g fiber, 267 mg sodium. Calories from fat: 22 percent.

 ## Potatoes with Leeks and Gruyere

This is a super dish for a holiday dinner—it can even be assembled a day in advance—just bake it on the big day. It can also be baked, cooled, covered, and refrigerated the day before. Just re-warm, covered, in 350-degree oven for about 25 minutes.

Makes 12 servings.

- 1 tbs. olive oil or canola oil.
- 1 lb. leeks (white and pale green parts only), thinly sliced.
- 8 oz. package of light cream cheese, room temperature.
- 1 tsp. salt.
- 1 tsp. ground black pepper.
- 1/4 tsp. ground nutmeg (more if desired).
- 1 cup low-fat milk.
- 1 large egg.
- 1/2 cup egg substitute.
- 2 lbs. frozen shredded hash browns, thawed somewhat.
- 2 cups grated Gruyere cheese (about 8 oz.).

- 1 tsp. of parsley flakes or Italian herb blend, or fines herbs.
1. Preheat oven to 350 degrees. Coat a 13-x9-x2-inch baking dish with canola cooking spray.
2. Add olive oil to large nonstick skillet over medium heat. Add leeks and sauté until tender (about 8 minutes). Remove from heat and set aside.
3. Blend cream cheese, salt, pepper, and nutmeg in food processor mixer. Slowly add milk and eggs one at a time, if using a mixer and beat just until blended. (Otherwise dump both the milk and eggs in the food processor and pulse just until blended). Stir leeks, shredded potatoes, and Gruyere into milk mixture and pour into prepared baking dish. Sprinkle parsley flakes or herb blend over the top if desired.
4. Bake dish until cooked through and top is brown (about 50–60 minutes). Cool slightly and serve.

Per serving: 217 calories, 11.5 g protein, 24 g carbohydrate, 8.5 g fat, 4.5 g saturated fat, 41 mg cholesterol, 2 g fiber, 340 mg sodium. Calories from fat: 35 percent.

Sour Creamed Potatoes

Makes 6 servings.

- 3 medium russet potatoes.
- 1 tbs. butter, canola margarine, or canola diet margarine.
- 5 tbs. fat-free or light sour cream.
- 3 tbs. low-fat milk.
- 1/2–1 tsp. minced or crushed garlic.

- 2 to 3 green onions, white and part of green, chopped.
- 1 1/2 tbs. fresh parsley, chopped.
- 6 tbs. grated or shredded Parmesan cheese.
- Add pepper to taste.
- Reduced-fat grated sharp cheddar cheese (optional).

1. Microwave or bake potatoes until tender throughout. Cut lengthwise in half. Scoop out as much of the potato from the skin as possible and put in a mixing bowl. (Set potato skins aside.)
2. To potato, add butter, sour cream, milk, garlic, onions, parsley, and Parmesan cheese. Blend with a mixer until creamy. Add pepper if desired.
3. Spoon into potato skins and sprinkle the top with grated cheese if desired. Broil until lightly brown.

Per serving: 163 calories, 6 g protein, 27 g carbohydrates, 3.5 g fat, 5 mg cholesterol, 2.5 g fiber, 159 mg sodium. Calories from fat: 19 percent.

 ## Creamy Green Bean Bake

Makes 6 servings.

- 4 cups lightly cooked French-style frozen green beans.
- 10 3/4-oz. can condensed Campbell's Healthy Request cream of mushroom soup (or similar).
- 1/2 cup fat-free or light sour cream.
- 1 tbs. diced pimento (optional).
- 1/4 cup canned chow mein fried noodles (in Asian food section of your supermarket).

1. Lightly cook frozen beans if you haven't already. Preheat oven to 350 degrees.
2. In a 1-quart casserole dish or 9-x-9-inch dish, combine condensed soup, sour cream, and pimento. Measure 4 cups of cooked green beans, add to dish, and stir.
3. Bake for 20 minutes or until bubbly. Sprinkle chow mein noodles over the top and bake 5 minutes more.

Per serving: 102 calories, 4 g protein, 16 g carbohydrate, 2 gram fat, 2 mg cholesterol, 3 g fiber, 337 mg sodium. Calories from fat: 20 percent.

 ## O'Brien Potato Casserole

Makes 16 servings.

- 2 lbs. Ore-Ida Potatoes O'Brien (about 8 cups).
- 2 cups fat-free or light sour cream.
- 6 green onions, white and part of green, finely chopped.
- 10 3/4-oz. can Campbell's Healthy Request cream of mushroom soup (or similar).
- 1/2 cup low-fat milk.
- 2 tbs. butter sprinkles (such as Molly McButter).
- 8 oz. shredded reduced-fat sharp cheddar cheese.
- 1/2 tsp. salt.
- 1/2 tsp. pepper.
- 2 oz. Reduced-fat Ruffles potato chips, crushed (optional).

1. Preheat oven to 325 degrees. Coat a 13-x9-inch baking pan with canola cooking spray.

2. Thaw potatoes and combine with all ingredients except the potato chips. Spread into prepared pan and top with crushed chips if desired. Bake for about 30 minutes.

Per serving: 115 calories, 7 g protein, 14.5 g carbohydrate, 3 g fat, 1 g fiber, 10 mg cholesterol, 308 mg sodium. Calories from fat: 26 percent.

 ## Apple Sweet Potato Bake

Makes 6 servings.

- Canola cooking spray.
- 5 cups thinly sliced sweet potatoes (or yams).
- 2 cups thinly sliced apples.
- 1/4 cup plus 2 tbs. brown sugar, packed.
- 2 tbs. maple syrup.
- 1/2 tsp. ground cinnamon.
- 1/2 cup apple juice.
- 4 tbs. chopped walnuts.

1. Preheat oven to 350 degrees. Coat a 9-x9-inch baking dish with canola cooking spray.
2. In a large bowl, toss the first three ingredients together. Spoon into the prepared baking dish.
3. In a small bowl, blend syrup with cinnamon. Add apple juice and stir to blend. Pour evenly over sweet potato mixture. Sprinkle walnuts over the top. Cover with foil and bake for 30 minutes.
4. Remove foil and bake about 20 minutes longer or until apple and sweet potatoes are cooked throughout.

Per serving: 193 calories, 2.5 g protein, 38.5 g carbohydrate, 3 g fat, 0 mg cholesterol, 3.5 g fiber, 14 mg sodium. Calories from fat: 15 percent.

Cranberry Walnut Dressing

Eliminate the onions if they are one of your heartburn trigger foods.

Makes about 16 (1 cup each) servings.

- 1 1/2 cups fincly sliced celery heart.
- 1 1/2 cups chopped onion (1 large onion).
- 3 tbs. butter or canola margarine.
- 1 cup reduced sodium chicken broth (liquid).
- 16 oz. can whole berry cranberry sauce.
- 4 tsp. or cubes of low sodium chicken broth (powder).
- 2 cups reduced sodium chicken broth (liquid).
- 3/4 tsp. ground sage.
- 1 tsp. thyme.
- 1/2 tsp. ground pepper.
- 14 oz. (about 8 cups) herb-seasoned bread cubes for stuffing.
- 2/3 cup walnuts, toasted for 1 minute under broiler to lightly brown.

1. In a Dutch oven or stock pot, simmer celery and onion in the butter and 1 cup chicken broth until tender.

2. While onion and celery mixture is simmering, in a small saucepan mix cranberry sauce with the 4 tsp. of chicken broth powder over low heat until broth powder dissolves.

3. Add seasonings and 2 cups chicken broth to celery-onion mixture. Add bread cubes and stir until evenly moistened. Drizzle cranberry mixture over the top of the bread mixture and sprinkle walnuts over cranberry mixture. Stir to mix evenly. Cover and let

sit on warm setting of stove for about 20 minutes, stirring occasionally.

Per serving: 200 calories, 4.5 g protein, 32.5 g carbohydrate, 5.8 g fat, 6 mg cholesterol, 415 mg sodium. Calories from fat: 26 percent.

Party Hints

You walk in and look around. As you are greeted, you try to remember if this is your third or fourth holiday party this week. You grab a handful of those cute-as-can-be Christmas M&Ms on your way to talk with a friend. While talking, you nibble on a couple handfuls of chips and dip and crackers and cheese. Later, you try pieces of English toffee and fudge sitting on the coffee table, on top of several toothpicks of fancy sausage that you had. By the time you walk out of the party, you have racked up a total of around 2,200 calories, most of which are from fat.

I'm not suggesting we all roam around our holiday parties drinking water and chewing on celery sticks. But we can save ourselves from post-party heartburn by partying with a little extra food wisdom. Start by taking the 10 Tips Toward a Heartburn-Free Holiday to heart. Then check out some of these heartburn-friendly appetizer recipes.

 Salmon Spread

Makes about 2 cups of spread.

- 7 1/2 oz. of freshly cooked salmon or smoked salmon.
- 1/2 cup light cream cheese.
- 1/4 cup part-skim or low-fat ricotta cheese.

- 1/3 cup (heaped) jicama or canned water chestnuts (well drained), finely chopped.
- 1/4 cup white onion, finely chopped (optional).
- 1 tbs. parsley flakes.
- 1/2 tsp. black pepper.
- 1 loaf French bread, cut into 16 slices.

1. Mix all ingredients (except bread), very briefly, in food processor. Stir the mixture around, scraping sides of food processor bowl, and briefly blend again. Keep well chilled (you can make this a day before you need it).
2. Spread one tbs. of spread on each 1/2 slice of bread.

Per 1/2 slice of bread: 59 calories, 3.5 g protein, 8 g carbohydrate, 1.5 g fat, .5 g saturated fat, 5 mg cholesterol, .5 g fiber, 105 mg sodium. Calories from fat: 22 percent.

 ## Crab Spread

Makes about 2 cups of spread.

- 6 oz. fresh crab, shredded.
- 1/2 cup light cream cheese, at room temperature.
- 1/4 cup plain yogurt.
- 1 tbs. onion flakes (optional).
- 1 tbs. parsley flakes.
- 1/2 tsp. black pepper.
- 1/8 tsp. salt.
- 1/3 cup chopped water chestnuts or jicama.
- Reduced-fat Ritz crackers (or similar).

1. Mix crab, cream cheese, yogurt, and seasonings together in mixer on low speed. Stir in water chestnuts or jicama.
2. Serve with reduced-fat crackers.

Per 1/8 cup of spread: 114 calories, 10 g protein, 4 g carbohydrate, 6.5 g fat, 3.5 g saturated fat, 36 mg cholesterol, .2 g fiber, 311 mg sodium. Calories from fat: 51 percent.

 ## Spinach Dip (in Sourdough Round)

Makes 12 appetizer servings.

- 1 round sourdough bread loaf (about 24 oz.).
- 1/3 cup real mayonnaise.
- 1 2/3 cup fat-free or light sour cream.
- 5 oz. can sliced water chestnuts, drained and chopped.
- 5 green onions, white and part of green, chopped (optional).
- 1 package leek, onion, or vegetable soup mix (such as Knorr Soup Mix).
- 10 oz. box frozen chopped spinach; thaw and squeeze out excess water.

1. Cut out top and center portion of sourdough round to make a bowl for the spinach dip. Cut the remaining bread into cubes for dipping.
2. In medium-sized bowl, blend mayonnaise and sour cream with soup mix powder. Stir in water chestnuts, onions if tolerated, and well-drained spinach.
3. Spread into sourdough bowl. Serve with bread cubes.

Per serving: 253 calories, 8 g protein, 39.5 g carbohydrate, 6.5 g fat, 1 g saturated fat, 4 mg cholesterol, 3 g fiber, 500 mg sodium. Calories from fat: 24 percent.

Class Crab Mold

Makes 16 spread servings.

- 8 oz. crab meat (fresh, frozen, or canned, drained well and patted dry).
- 1 can Campbell's Healthy Request cream of mushroom soup (or similar).
- 1 envelope Knox plain, unflavored gelatin.
- 8 oz. light cream cheese.
- 1/4 cup real mayonnaise.
- 3/4 cup fat-free or light sour cream.
- 1/2 cup chopped green onions (if tolerated).
- 1 cup finely chopped celery.
- **Serving suggestion:** serve with thinly sliced French or sourdough baguette, water crackers, or other low-fat crackers.

1. Heat concentrated cream of mushroom soup in medium saucepan over medium-low heat. Add gelatin and cream cheese and let it come to a gentle boil. Let boil, stirring frequently, until cream cheese melts and gelatin dissolves. Remove from heat.

2. Stir in mayonnaise, sour cream, crab, green onions if tolerated, and celery. Spread into 1 quart mold or larger, and refrigerate until set.

Per serving (spread only): 84 calories, 6 g protein, 4 g carbohydrate, 5 g fat, 1.5 g saturated fat, 21 mg cholesterol, .2 g fiber, 258 mg sodium. Calories from fat: 54 percent.

A holiday bonus for you!

With these "light" renditions of favorite holiday foods eaten in reasonable amounts, there is no acid reflux reason why we all can't enjoy holiday foods once a month instead of just once a year!

Chapter 6

Recipes You
Can't Live Without

What types of recipes would be helpful in a book about acid reflux? Tums Tacos or Pepcid AC Cookies? No, take another gander at the 10 Food Steps to Freedom (Chapter 3) and a few patterns emerge.

I've come up with some no-tomato options to our top tomato dishes (and eliminated the garlic and onion, too, when possible). Please forgive me but I couldn't come up with a no-tomato way of making spaghetti. I guess you could use a type of gravy instead of marinara sauce, but then that would be beef stroganoff wouldn't it? I've even looked at 10 popular fatty foods and lightened them up so that you will eat fried chicken again!

Why is it so important to lighten up some of America's most fatty foods? (Other than the fact that food fat delays the emptying of the stomach into the small intestine, helps relax or weaken the esophageal sphincter valve, and a high-fat diet encourages weight gain.) When do people tend to have the most trouble with acid reflux? When they eat out.

What have studies shown happens when people eat out? They eat a higher amount of fat (not to mention cholesterol and sodium, too). So I looked at the favorite foods people eat when they eat breakfast out:

- Eggs.
- Pancakes.

I also looked at the favorite foods people eat when they eat lunch or dinner out:

- Lettuce salads.
- French fries.
- Mashed potatoes.
- Coleslaw.
- Pizza.
- Pasta.
- Chocolate chip cookies.

I included lower-fat versions of as many of the above items as I possibly could. Because if you enjoy these items enough to order them when you are out at the mall or in a restaurant, then you are bound to enjoy and appreciate these same foods when they are made lighter at home.

In the recipes below, just to keep the bases covered, obviously I've tried to honor the 10 Food Steps to Freedom whenever possible. Keep in mind everyone is going to be a little different. Some people have to eat spicy foods or high tomato recipes with caution, while others find the greasy, fatty foods particularly problematic. Hopefully, no matter which food step to freedom you find gives the most relief, there will be a handful of recipes in this chapter that will help, not hurt, your heartburn.

No-tomato recipes
for top tomato dishes

 ## No-Tomato Lasagna
(Creamy Pesto Lasagna)

Make up a batch of white sauce and you're ready to throw
this recipe together.

Makes 12 servings.

- 12 oz. (3/4 lb.) super lean ground beef (or
  ground sirloin).
- 1/3 cup (2.5 oz.) pesto (I use Armanino Pesto in
  the frozen food section).
- 1/2 cup beef broth.
- 2 cups grated zucchini.
- 1 1/2 cup part-skim ricotta cheese.
- 2/3 cup chopped green onions (if tolerated).
- 12 oz. (dry weight) wide lasagna noodles.
- 2 cups low-fat white sauce (see following
  recipe).
- 6 oz. grated part-skim mozzarella cheese
  (1 1/2 cups).

1. Preheat oven to 375 degrees. Cook noodles in a large
   pot of boiling water until just tender (follow cooking
   directions on package). Drain well.

2. While boiling noodles, in nonstick frying pan coated
   with canola cooking spray, brown ground beef—
   breaking into small pieces with spatula as it cooks.
   Add browned beef to large bowl along with pesto,
   broth, and zucchini. Toss to blend well.

3. In a separate bowl, mix the ricotta with green
   onions.

4. To assemble lasagna:
   - Spread 1 cup of white sauce on bottom of 9-x-13-x-2-inch baking pan.
   - Add 3 strips of lasagna noodles.
   - Spread half of the beef mixture on top.
   - Lay 3 strips of lasagna over the beef.
   - Spread the ricotta cheese mixture on top.
   - Add 3 strips of lasagna.
   - Spread the remaining beef mixture on top of this.
   - Add 3 strips of lasagna.
   - Spread the very top with remaining white sauce.
   - Sprinkle with the grated mozzarella

Per serving: 318 calories, 19.5 g protein, 27 g carbohydrate, 14.5 g fat, 7 g saturated fat, 41 mg cholesterol, 1.5 g fiber, 316 mg sodium. Calories from fat: 40 percent.

 ## Easy Low-fat Alfredo Sauce

This is a sauce recipe for the Creamy Pesto Lasagna recipe above, but it is a great entrée in it's own right. Just toss the sauce with roasted chicken breast strips, cooked prawns, or crumbled turkey bacon, and drizzle over cooked noodles and you've got a marvelous variation of fettuccine alfredo!

Makes about 2 cups.

- 1/4 cup light cream cheese.
- 1 1/4 cup low-fat or whole milk, divided.
- 1 tbs. Wondra quick-mixing flour.
- 2 tbs. butter (canola margarine can also be used), divided.

- 1/2 cup shredded Parmesan cheese.
- Add salt and freshly grated pepper to taste.
- Add nutmeg to taste.

1. Combine cream cheese, 1/4 cup whole milk, and flour in a small mixing bowl or food processor. Beat or pulse until well blended. Slowly pour in remaining milk (1 cup) and beat until smooth.
2. Melt 2 tbs. butter in large, thick nonstick frying pan or saucepan over medium heat. Add the milk mixture and continue to heat, stirring constantly, until the sauce is just the right thickness (about 4 minutes).
3. Stir in grated Parmesan cheese and add salt, pepper, and nutmeg to taste if desired.

Per serving: If each 1/3 cup of sauce is served with 1 cup of cooked fettuccine noodles. 333 calories, 13 g protein, 43.5 g carbohydrate, 11.5 g fat, 6 g saturated fat, 31 mg cholesterol, 2 g fiber, 250 mg sodium. Calories from fat: 31 percent.

 ## No-Tomato Pizza

**Makes 2 servings
(each serving is half a small pizza).**

- 1 small packaged (ready-to-bake) pizza crust (5.5 oz.) such as Boboli brand or other.
- 2 tbs. prepared pesto sauce (such as Armanino in frozen food section) or quick ranch sauce (blend 1/8 cup fat-free or light sour cream with 1/2 tsp. Hidden Valley Ranch Dip powder from packet).
- 1/2 cup grated reduced-fat cheese (mozzarella, sharp cheddar, Jack, or a blend).

- 1/2 cup of toppings you know you can tolerate, (such as a mixture of mushrooms, zucchini, lean ham, and pineapple, etc.).

1. Preheat oven to 400 degrees.
2. Place pizza crust on cookie sheet. Spread pesto or quick ranch sauce evenly over the crust. Top evenly with grated cheese then the toppings of your choice.
3. Bake 8–12 minutes or until cheese is melted and crust lightly browned. Cut pizza in half.

Per serving (using pesto and zucchini and mushroom as the topping): 316 calories, 14.5 g protein, 36 g carbohydrate, 12 g fat, 4 g saturated fat, 18 mg cholesterol, 3 g fiber, 580 mg sodium. Calories from fat: 35 percent.

10-Minute Spaghetti Carbonara (no-egg-yolk version)

I was trying to think of a way of making spaghetti but without tomatoes and I thought it was mission impossible, but then I remembered my recipe for spaghetti Carbonara!

Makes 3 servings (2–4).

- 4 cups cooked spaghetti noodles (until tender, but still a little firm), drained.
- 1/4 cup egg substitute.
- 1 tbs. Wondra quick-mixing flour.
- 1/2 cup plus 2 tbs. double strength chicken broth.
- 1/4 cup dry white cooking wine
- 2 garlic cloves, minced—about 2 tsp. (if tolerated).
- 2 tbs. butter.
- Salt and freshly ground pepper (optional).

- 4 slices Louis Rich turkey bacon, cooked carefully over medium-low heat and crumbled.
- 2/3 cup freshly grated Parmesan cheese.

1. Boil spaghetti noodles if you haven't already done so. In a small bowl, blend egg substitute with the Wondra flour; set aside.
2. In large nonstick skillet, combine the chicken broth, wine, garlic, and butter. Bring the mixture to a boil. Let boil gently for a minute or two. Turn off the heat. Season mixture with salt and pepper if desired.
3. Turn off heat. Add in the egg substitute mixture, stir well. Add the warm spaghetti noodles and toss well.
4. Stir in the crumbled turkey bacon and parmesan cheese and toss well.

Per serving: 396 calories, 18 g protein, 45 g carbohydrate, 14.5 g fat, 7.5 g saturated fat, 40 mg cholesterol, 2.5 g fiber, 860 mg sodium. Calories from fat: 35 percent.

 ## Green Sauced Chicken Enchiladas

The green sauce in this recipe is made with tomatillos. Tomatillos are generally thought of as green Mexican tomatoes, but they are really botanically different from tomatoes. If you find you can tolerate tomatillos, then you have a simple solution to your favorite Mexican foods. Bottled salsa verde (made with tomatillos) can be used as salsa and sauce and substituted for salsa or enchilada sauce in most recipes.

Makes 6 servings (2 enchiladas each).

- 4 chicken breasts, boneless and skinless (1 lb.).

- Chicken broth (enough to cover chicken—about 2–4 cups).
- 2/3 cup chopped green onions, white and part of green (if tolerated).
- 8 oz. grated reduced-fat Monterey Jack or cheddar cheese (or a mixture).
- 12 corn or flour tortillas. ·
- 1/4 cup milk or chicken broth.
- 1 cup of bottled mild salsa verde (made with tomatillos, onions, some peppers, salt, and cilantro).
- 1 cup fat-free or light sour cream.

1. Add chicken breasts to a medium saucepan and add enough chicken broth to cover. Bring to a boil, then reduce heat to a simmer until cooked throughout (about 20 minutes). Let cool in chicken broth. Shred with hands and toss in a medium bowl with onion if tolerated, and the grated cheese.

2. Preheat oven to 375 degrees. Coat a 13-x9-x2-inch baking pan with canola cooking spray.

3. One by one, heat tortillas in a nonstick frying pan until softened. Lay about 1/3 cup of chicken mixture down the center of each tortilla. Add a tsp. of milk or chicken broth down the center, roll up, and place seamside down in the baking pan.

4. Cover the pan with foil and bake for 20–30 minutes.

5. Add salsa verde and sour cream to a mixing bowl and beat on low with mixer (or by hand) until combined. Spoon green sauce over the chicken enchiladas before serving, then pass any remaining sauce around the table.

Per serving (using flour tortillas): 470 calories, 35.5 g protein, 51 g carbohydrate, 13 g fat, 5 g saturated fat,

70 mg cholesterol, 2 g fiber, 715 mg sodium. Calories from fat: 25 percent.

 ## Mock Veal Parmesan

Makes 4 servings.

- 4 chicken breasts, boneless and skinless.
- 1/2 cup egg substitute.
- 1 cup Italian seasoned bread crumbs (plain can also be used).
- 1/2 tsp. garlic powder (if tolerated).
- 1 tsp. Italian herb seasoning.
- 1 tsp. parsley flakes.
- 1 tbs. canola oil.
- 1 cup carrot sauce (see recipe below).
- 4 oz. part skim or reduced-fat grated mozzarella cheese
- **Serving suggestion:** Serve each chicken breast over 3/4 cup cooked fettuccini noodles.

1. Preheat oven to 350 degrees.
2. Place a chicken breast between two sheets of waxed paper. Pound the side of the chicken breast that used to have the skin with a meat mallet until it's about 1/4-inch thick (or even better, ask your butcher to do it for you).
3. Pour egg substitute in a small shallow bowl. In another bowl, blend bread crumbs, garlic powder (if tolerated), herb seasoning, and parsley. Dip each breast in egg substitute then coat well with bread-crumb mixture.
4. Spread canola oil evenly over the bottom of a 9-x-9-inch baking dish. Place chicken breasts in pan. Bake for 20 minutes. Spread at least 1/4 cup of carrot

sauce over each breast. Then sprinkle mozzarella cheese over the tops and bake another 10 minutes or until chicken is cooked throughout and cheese is melted. Serve over cooked noodles if desired.

Per serving: 416 calories, 42 g protein, 26 g carbohydrate, 15 g fat, 5.5 g saturated fat, 95 mg cholesterol, 2 g fiber, 1150 mg sodium. Calories from fat: 32 percent.

 Carrot Sauce

Makes about 1 1/2 cups of sauce.

- 1 1/2 cups finely grated carrots.
- 1/2 cup low-fat or whole milk.
- 1 tbs. butter or canola margarine.
- 2 tsp. cornstarch.
- 4 tbs. low-fat or whole milk, divided.
- 3 tbs. Parmesan cheese.
- 1/2 tsp. oregano.
- Pepper to taste.

1. Puree grated carrots in blender or food processor with 1/2 cup milk. Melt butter on medium heat in large nonstick frying pan. Add carrot mixture and let bubble for a minute.
2. In small dish, blend 2 tsp. cornstarch with 2 tbs. of the milk until smooth. Blend in remaining 2 tbs. of the milk. Add to the carrot mixture, stir frequently, and let bubble a few minutes more. Reduce heat to simmer. Sprinkle cheese and spices on top, stir, and let simmer several minutes.

Light Versions of 10 Fatty Foods
Favorite breakfast foods

 Buttermilk Pancakes

Starting the day off with a stack of rich pancakes, piled high with scoops of butter, all aside three greasy sausage links, can send your acid reflux into overload. Start the day off instead with a couple of light buttermilk pancakes, a nice drizzle of syrup, and two lean links of sausage and you'll be well on your way to a heartburn-free day.

Makes 5 servings (about 3–4 pancakes each).

- 2 cups cake flour.
- 2 tsp. baking powder.
- 1 tsp. baking soda.
- 1/2 tsp. salt.
- 2 tbs. sugar.
- 2 large eggs.
- 2 cups buttermilk (low-fat).
- 1 tsp. vanilla.
- 2 tbs. butter, melted.
- 1/4 cup reduced-calorie pancake syrup.
- **Serving suggestion:** serve each stack of pancakes with a couple of less-fat sausage links or patties (such as Jimmy Dean Lite Sausage with 50 percent less fat) and a small bowl of fresh fruit.

1. Combine flour, baking powder, baking soda, salt, and sugar in medium bowl and blend well with fork.
2. Beat eggs, buttermilk, and vanilla in mixing bowl on medium-low speed until smooth.

3. Add melted butter, pancake syrup, and dry ingredients to egg mixture in mixing bowl and beat on lowest speed, scraping with rubber spatula, just until blended. Do not overmix.

4. Let batter rest for 20 minutes. Spray griddle lightly with canola cooking spray. Preheat griddle until water skittles.

5. Pour 1/4 cup batter onto griddle. Cook over medium heat until bubbles form in pancake (30 to 60 seconds). Turn over with spatula and cook another 30 to 60 seconds or until golden brown

Per serving: 292 calories, 9 g protein, 46 g carbohydrate, 7.5 g fat, 4 g saturated fat, 100 mg cholesterol, 1 g fiber, 870 mg sodium. Calories from fat: 24 percent.

 ## Light Denver Omelet

These omelets are great paired with the oil-free hash browns (recipe below).

Makes 2 fluffy omelets.

- 1 cup sliced fresh mushrooms.
- 1 medium green pepper, chopped (as tolerated).
- 4 green onions, sliced diagonally (as tolerated).
- 1/4 tsp. dried basil, crushed.
- 1/2 cup chicken broth.
- 1/2 cup very lean ham cut into 1-inch-long strips (about 2 oz.).
- 1/2 cup cherry tomatoes, halved.
- 1/2 cup egg substitute.
- 2 eggs, separated.
- Canola cooking spray.

1. Start heating a medium nonstick frying pan over medium heat and coat with canola cooking spray. Add sliced mushrooms, green pepper, green onions, and basil. Sauté about 20 seconds, then pour in 1/2 cup chicken broth and cook, stirring frequently, until tender. Stir in ham and cherry tomatoes and set mixture aside.

2. Blend egg substitute and egg yolks together in medium-sized bowl and set aside. With mixer, beat egg whites until stiff. Carefully fold egg whites into egg-yolk mixture.

3. Generously coat a nonstick omelet pan or small frying pan with canola cooking spray and heat over medium heat. Spread half of egg mixture in pan. Heat until top looks firm (about 2 minutes). If your pan cooks hotter than normal, cook over low heat. Flip omelet over to lightly brown other side (about 1 minute). Fill with vegetable-ham filling, and fold as desired. Remove to serving plate.

4. Repeat with remaining egg mixture.

Per serving: 188 calories, 22 g protein, 9 g carbohydrate, 7 g fat, 229 mg cholesterol, 2 g fiber, 690 mg sodium. Calories from fat: 34 percent.

 ## Oil-free Hash Browns

Makes 2 servings.

- 2 cups frozen Southern Style Hash Browns (or 2 cups red potatoes, chopped in 1/3-inch cubes).
- 1 1/2 cups chicken broth (low sodium).
- 1/2 cup chopped onion (if tolerated).
- 1 or 2 cloves garlic (if tolerated).
- 1 tbs. parsley flakes.

- **Optional:** 1/3 cup grated reduced-fat sharp cheddar cheese.

1. Heat broth, onion, garlic, parsley, and potatoes in medium saucepan until boiling.
2. Reduce heat to low and let simmer, uncovered, until water evaporates and potatoes are tender (about 15 minutes).
3. Add cheese if desired.

Per serving (with cheese): 255 calories, 10 g protein, 39.5 g carbohydrate, 6 g fat, 20 mg cholesterol, 220 mg sodium. Calories from fat: 22 percent.

 ## Ham Skillet Breakfast

Makes one large serving.

- 1 medium boiling potato.
- 1 egg.
- 1/4 cup egg substitute.
- 1 tbs. low-fat milk.
- 1 tbs. finely chopped parsley (or 1 tsp. dried parsley flakes).
- 1/4 tsp. salt (optional).
- Freshly ground pepper (as tolerated).
- Canola cooking spray.
- 1/4 cup finely chopped onions (as tolerated).
- 1/4 cup finely diced lean ham.
- Water (if needed).

1. With fork, pierce the potato three times. Place it on a microwave-safe dish and microwave on high until tender (about 7 minutes). Set aside to cool.
2. With a plastic knife, peel the potato (if desired) and cut the potato into 1/4-inch slices; set aside.

3. In a medium bowl, beat the egg, egg substitute, milk, parsley, salt (if desired), and a few grindings of pepper with a fork until they are well blended.

4. Coat a nonstick skillet with canola cooking spray. Add the onion and ham and cook, stirring frequently with the spatula, over medium heat until onion is soft but not brown (about 5 minutes). Add a 1/4 cup of water if moisture is needed.

5. Add the potato slices to the onion/ham mixture and cook, turning occasionally with the spatula, over medium-low heat until they are light brown (about 5 minutes). Add 1/4 cup of water if moisture is needed.

6. Pour in the egg mixture. Tip the pan from side to side to spread the egg evenly. Reduce the heat to low and cook, without stirring, for 5 minutes. With the spatula, scoop up the underside of the mixture several times to prevent the eggs from sticking.

7. When the eggs are set, invert a serving plate over the skillet and, grasping the skillet and plate firmly together, quickly turn them over.

Per Serving: 383 calories, 23 g protein, 57 g carbohydrate, 6.8 g fat, 2 g saturated fat, 225 mg cholesterol, 5.5 g fiber, 590 mg sodium. Calories from fat: 16 percent.

Favorite side dishes for lunch or dinner

 ## Macaroni Salad for Purists

This is a no-frills recipe for macaroni salad. But because of its simplicity, it is real easy to make and appeals to kids and discerning grown-ups alike.

Makes 8 side servings.

- 3 hard-boiled eggs.
- 2 cups dry macaroni.
- 3 green onions, white and part of green, finely chopped.
- 2 tsp. parsley flakes, or 2 tbs. fresh, finely chopped parsley.
- 1/4 tsp. salt.
- Freshly ground pepper to taste.
- 2 tbs. real mayonnaise.
- 1/4 cup light or fat-free sour cream.

1. Start boiling your eggs if you haven't done this already. Then boil the macaroni noodles following directions on box (boil about 8–10 minutes). Drain noodles well and rinse with cold water and let cool.
2. Place noodles in serving bowl along with green onions, parsley, salt, and pepper to taste. In small bowl, blend mayonnaise with sour cream; add mayonnaise mixture to the noodles in serving bowl.
3. Peel shells off eggs and remove 2 of the cooked yolks (discard other yolks). Chop remaining eggs and stir into macaroni mixture. Add more salt and pepper if needed to taste. Let sit in refrigerator overnight (if you've got time).

Per serving: 145 calories, 5.5 g protein, 21.5 g carbohydrate, 3.8 g fat, .7 g saturated fat, 28 mg cholesterol, 1 g fiber, 128 mg sodium. Calories from fat: 24 percent.

 ## Spicy Steak Fries

Once you've tried these, you won't go back to deep-fried again. If you don't tolerate seasoning salt well, add salt and any herb blends that you like in its place.

Makes 6 servings.

- 4 medium to large russet (baking) potatoes.
- 1 tbs. canola oil.
- Canola cooking spray.
- 1/2 tsp. seasoning salt and add more to taste.

1. Scrub the potatoes and cut them crosswise in half. Place cut-side down on a cutting board and use an apple cutter/corer to cut into wedges. Or an adult can use a sharp knife to cut into steak fries. If time permits, soak the potatoes in cold water for up to 1 hour to remove excess starch; drain and dry well.

2. Preheat oven to 425 degrees. Coat the bottom of a 9-x-13-inch baking pan or small cookie sheet with 1 tbs. of canola oil.

3. Place the potato wedges in the pan. Spray the tops of the fries generously with canola cooking spray. Bake for about 20 minutes. Flip the fries over, sprinkle with salt, and bake for 10 minutes more, until lightly browned.

Per serving: 203 calories, 3.5 g protein, 41.5 g carbohydrate, 2.4 g fat, 0 g saturated fat, 0 mg cholesterol, 4 g fiber, 204 mg sodium. Calories from fat: 11 percent.

 ## Mock KFC Coleslaw

Makes 8 side servings.

- 1/3 cup sugar.
- 1/2 tsp. salt.
- 1/8 tsp. freshly ground pepper (if tolerated).
- 1/4 cup low-fat milk (whole milk can be substituted).

- 2 tbs. real mayonnaise.
- 6 tbs. fat-free or light sour cream.
- 1/4 cup low-fat buttermilk.
- 1 1/2 tbs. white vinegar (seasoned rice vinegar can be substituted).
- 2 1/2 tbs. lemon juice.
- 8 cups finely chopped or shredded cabbage (about 1 medium head).
- 1 cup grated carrots.

1. In a large mixing bowl, combine the sugar, salt, pepper, milk, mayonnaise, sour cream, buttermilk, vinegar, and lemon juice and beat on low speed until smooth.
2. Add cabbage and carrots, and toss to blend with dressing. Cover and refrigerate until served.

Per serving: 99 calories, 2.5 g protein, 17 g carbohydrate, 3 g fat, .5 g saturated fat, 3 mg cholesterol, 2 g fiber, 190 mg sodium. Calories from fat: 27 percent.

Favorite entrées for lunch or dinner

Southern Fried Chicken (oven fried, that is)

Fried chicken is one of America's all-time favorite fried foods. So, of course, I couldn't talk about lightening 10 fatty foods without including it. This is a nice, mildly spiced recipe. If you want to crank up the seasonings, add 1 tsp. of Creole or Cajun seasoning (if you tolerate this well).

Makes 4 servings.

- 4 chicken breasts, skinless (with bone or boneless as desired).

- 1 cup low-fat buttermilk.
- 1–2 tsp. canola oil (for greasing bottom of baking sheet).
- 1 cup unbleached flour.
- 2 tsp. fresh cracked black pepper.
- 2 tsp. kosher salt (regular salt will work too)
- 1/4 tsp. cayenne pepper.
- Canola cooking spray.

1. Wash the chicken pieces and dry well with paper towels. Place the chicken in a gallon-size Ziploc bag and pour the buttermilk over the chicken. Seal the bag well and refrigerate for at least 30 minutes.

2. Preheat oven to 400 degrees. Add 1 to 2 tsp. of canola oil to cover bottom of a 9-x-9-x-2-inch baking dish.

3. Place the flour, pepper, salt, and cayenne pepper in another gallon-size Ziploc bag and shake to blend the ingredients.

4. Drain the chicken pieces briefly, then place one piece at a time in the bag filled with seasoned flour. Shake the bag vigorously to coat the chicken well; place chicken in prepared baking dish.

5. Coat the top of the chicken pieces with a generous coat of canola oil spray. Bake in center of oven for 20 to 25 minutes or until the chicken is nicely browned on the outside and cooked throughout on the inside.

Per serving (using 1 tsp. of canola oil to coat pan): 215 calories, 29.5 g protein, 13 g carbohydrate, 4 g fat, .6 g saturated fat, .5 g fiber, 69 mg cholesterol, 600 mg sodium. Calories from fat: 18 percent.

Beef Flautas

In Spanish, *flauta* means "flute." These meat-filled tortillas are rolled up like a flute and deep-fried until crispy. In this recipe we are oven frying the flautas until crispy, and using a lot less oil.

Makes 6 long flutes.

- 1 lb. extra-lean ground beef.
- 1 medium onion, chopped.
- 1 tsp. bottled minced garlic.
- 1 1/2 tsp. chili powder.
- 1 tsp. dry oregano leaves.
- 1/2 tsp. paprika.
- 1/4 tsp. ground cumin.
- 1/4 tsp. pepper.
- 2 tsp. Worcestershire sauce.
- 1/2 cup mild chili sauce (or canned tomato sauce).
- 12 corn tortillas.
- Canola cooking spray.
- **Serving suggestion:** guacamole (and mild salsa if tolerated well).

1. Preheat the oven to 400 degrees. In the skillet, place the ground beef, onion, and garlic. Brown the ground beef over medium-high heat, crumbling the meat into small pieces, using the spatula, as it cooks.

2. Add the chili powder, oregano, paprika, cumin, pepper, Worcestershire sauce, and chili sauce to the browned beef and stir.

3. Place 6 of the corn tortillas at a time into a damp kitchen towel and warm them in the microwave

on medium for about 2 minutes. (If you don't have a microwave, you will need to heat one tortilla at a time in an ungreased frying pan over medium heat until flexible, about 15 seconds per side.)

4. For each flauta, spray both sides of 2 tortillas lightly with canola cooking spray. Lay the tortillas down so they overlap by 4 inches. Spoon 1/4 cup of filling down the middle of the paired tortillas and roll up tightly. Place on thick cookie sheet. Bake the flautas in the preheated oven until the tortillas are crisp (15 minutes).

Per serving (1 flauta): 248 calorics, 15.5 g protein, 32.5 g carbohydrate, 6.5 g fat, 4 g fiber, 20 mg cholesterol, 280 mg sodium. Calories from fat: 24 percent.

 ## Mini Corn Tamales

Traditionally, tamales are wrapped in soaked cornhusks and steamed. But to make this recipe quick and easy for you to make, the tamales are wrapped in squares of foil. Make a batch, then unwrap the cooled leftover tamales, and keep them in a Ziploc bag in the freezer. For a quick lunch or dinner, just take out as many tamales as you need from the freezer and warm them up in the microwave (about 4 minutes for 2 tamales).

Makes 24 mini tamales.

- 2 cups *masa harina* (corn tortilla flour).
- 1 1/4 cups chicken broth (double strength if possible).
- 1/2 tsp. salt (optional).
- 3 tbs. canola oil.
- 1/4 cup nonfat or light sour cream.

- 2 cups finely shredded roasted or barbecued skinless chicken breast.
- 2 1/4-oz. can sliced or chopped olives (optional).
- 1 medium onion, finely chopped (if tolerated).
- 1/2 cup bottled enchilada sauce or green or red salsa (if tolerated).
- Boiling water.

Note: If tomato or tomatillo products are not tolerated well, use 1/2 cup of a gravy in place of the enchilada sauce or salsa.

1. Make 24 pieces of foil: Pull a strip of foil out of the box about 6 inches and carefully tear. Cut this in half to make two squares from the rectangle. Do this 11 more times to make 24 squares.

2. In a large mixing bowl, measure and combine the masa harina, chicken broth, salt (if desired), oil, and sour cream. With the electric mixer, beat briefly to make a thick paste. Spread 1 heaping tbs. of the paste in the shape of a 3-inch square in the center of each piece of foil.

3. In another bowl, combine the chicken, olives, and onion. Add the enchilada sauce or salsa (or gravy) and with the large spoon, toss everything together. Spoon a heaping tbs. of the chicken filling into the center of each masa square. Fold the foil edges together so the masa edges meet. Wrap the long end of the foil around each other and twist the ends.

4. Place a wire rack in a saucepan and pour in boiling water to a depth of 1 inch. The water should not reach the tamales; if the rack is too low, rest it on 2 small cans. Stack the tamales on the rack, arranging them loosely so steam can circulate. Bring to a boil, cover, and adjust the heat to keep the water

at a steady boil. Continue to cook, adding boiling water to maintain the water level, until the masa is nicely firm and does not stick to foil (test one from the center of the pan after 1 hour of steaming).

Per serving (2 mini tamales): 161 calories, 10 g protein, 17.5 g carbohydrate, 5.5 g fat, 2.5 g fiber, 20 mg cholesterol, 190 mg sodium. Calories from fat: 32 percent.

5 desserts that have nothing to do with chocolate and peppermint

 ## Key Lime Bars

I'm a lemon bar and key lime pie lover from way back. So, it took me mere minutes to work up a lighter version of this key lime bar recipe. I love the idea of marrying the classic lemon bar recipe with a key lime pie. I was worried though, that I would be disappointed after this big build up of taste expectation. Not to worry; these key lime bars are so yummy. The shortbread cookie crust was tender and tasty and the lime topping was just the right amount of tart and tang.

Makes 12 large or 24 small bars.

- 3 tbs. butter, softened.
- 3 tbs. light or fat-free cream cheese.
- 1/2 cup granulated sugar.
- 1 egg yolk.
- 3/4 cup unbleached flour.
- 2 tbs. powdered sugar.

- 1 egg.
- 1/4 cup egg substitute.
- 1 cup granulated sugar.
- 2 tbs. unbleached flour.
- 1/3 cup key lime juice (regular lime juice may be substituted).
- 2 tbs. powdered sugar (for sprinkling or sifting on top before serving).

1. Preheat oven to 350 degrees. Coat 8-x-8-x-2-inch baking dish with canola cooking spray.

2. In electric mixer, beat the butter, cream cheese, and 1/2 cup of sugar until light and fluffy. Beat in the egg yolk and gradually add the 3/4 cup flour. Spread into the prepared 8-x-8-inch pan. Sprinkle powdered sugar on top of the dough so the dough doesn't stick to the palm of your hands as you pat it down to make a crust in pan. Bake 15 minutes.

3. Meanwhile, in mixing bowl (you can use the same one you used to make the crust), beat the egg and egg substitute slightly. Add in 1 cup of sugar and 2 tbs. flour and beat on low speed until blended. Add the lime juice and beat on low until blended. Pour onto warm shortbread crust and bake for 15 minutes more.

4. Place on rack to cool. Before slicing and serving, sprinkle the top with 2 tbs. or more of sifted powdered sugar.

Per large bar (if 12 bars per recipe): 180 calories, 2.6 g protein, 33 g carbohydrate, 4.5 g fat, 2.5 g saturated fat, 45 mg cholesterol, .3 g fiber, 55 mg sodium. Calories from fat: 22 percent.

Creamy Cherry Pie

This pie was a breeze to make. No pastry pie crust to blend and roll (you make a graham cracker crust). And the filling just calls for 4 ingredients, 3 of which are extremely convenient (sweetened condensed milk, a carton of sour cream, and a can of cherry pie filling). About the only thing you have to do is squeeze a couple of lemons. But if you buy bottled lemon juice, you don't even have to do that!

Makes 12 servings.

Crust:

- 1 tbs. butter or canola margarine, melted.
- 2 tbs. fat-free or light sour cream.
- 1 tbs. lemon or orange liqueur (Grand Marnier or Caravella).
- 1 1/4-cup graham cracker crumbs.

Filling:

- 14 oz. can fat-free sweetened condensed milk.
- 1/4 cup lemon juice.
- 1 cup of fat-free or light sour cream.
- 21 oz. can of cherry pie filling.

1. Preheat oven to 400 degrees. Coat the bottom and sides of a 9-inch deep-dish pie plate with canola cooking spray.

2. Combine butter, 2 tbs. fat-free sour cream and lemon or orange liqueur in a food processor and pulse briefly just until blended. (If you don't have a food processor, blend the sour cream, liqueur, and butter together in a cup until smooth then drizzle it over the graham cracker crumbs in a medium bowl and stir well until completely blended.) Press

mixture in bottom and partway up the sides of a 9-inch pie plate and set aside.

3. Add sweetened condensed milk, lemon juice, and 1 cup of fat-free sour cream to mixing bowl and beat on low until smooth and creamy. Spread mixture over prepared crust.

4. Spoon cherry pie filling over cream mixture using small dinner spoons. Bake for about 18 minutes or until filling appears to be nicely set. Let cool for about 30, minutes then refrigerate to cool completely. When ready, cut into 12 wedges.

Per serving: 239 calories, 5 g protein, 49 g carbohydrate, 2.3 g fat, 1 g saturated fat, 3 mg cholesterol, .7 g fiber, 140 mg sodium. Calories from fat: 9 percent.

 ## Snickerdoodles

I know chocolate chip cookies are the most popular cookie, but if you are avoiding chocolate—snickerdoodles have got to be a close second. They stay moist for days but I highly recommend you try them fresh from the oven.

Makes 3 dozen.

- 1/2 cup butter.
- 1/4 cup light corn syrup.
- 1/4 cup light cream cheese (in block).
- 1 1/4 cup white sugar.
- 1 egg.
- 2 egg whites.
- 2 tsp. double-strength vanilla extract (regular can be used).

- 2 3/4 cup unbleached flour.
- 2 tsp. cream of tartar.
- 1 tsp. baking soda.
- 1/4 tsp. salt.
- 3 tbs. white sugar.
- 3 tsp. ground cinnamon.

1. Preheat oven to 400 degrees. Coat a thick cookie sheet with canola cooking spray.
2. Cream together butter, corn syrup, cream cheese, 1 1/4 cups sugar in mixer on medium speed. Add the egg, egg whites, and the vanilla and beat until blended.
3. Add the flour, cream of tartar, soda, and salt to mixing bowl. Beat on low speed to form a dough. Refrigerate for 2 hours or until firm enough to handle.
4. Add 3 tbs. sugar and cinnamon to small, shallow bowl and blend well.
5. Use a cookie scoop (1/8 level cup or heaping tbs.) to form cookie balls and roll each generously in the cinnamon sugar mixture. Place on cookie sheet, 2 inches apart. Bake about 8 minutes or until set, but not too hard. Remove immediately from cookie sheet.

Per cookie: 99 calories, 1.5 g protein, 17 g carbohydrate, 2.9 g fat, 1.7 g saturated fat, 13 mg cholesterol, .3 g fiber, 90 mg sodium. Calories from fat: 26 percent.

 ## Raspberry Coconut Bars

Raspberry bars—not to be confused with the more famous lemon bars. These bars have coconut and chopped pecans and are topped with a thin baked meringue-type topping.

I couldn't even tell the light rendition of these bars were light. I love this recipe!

Makes 24 bars.

- 6 tbs. butter, softened.
- 6 tbs. light cream cheese.
- 1 1/2 cups sugar.
- 2 eggs, separated.
- 1 1/2 cups all-purpose flour.
- 3/4 cup raspberry preserves (you can buy seedless or less sugar types if you prefer).
- 1/2 cup shredded coconut.
- 3/4 cup chopped pecans.

1. Preheat oven to 350 degrees. Coat a 13-x9-x2-inch baking pan with canola cooking spray.

2. In electric mixer, beat the butter, cream cheese, and 1 cup of sugar until light and fluffy. Beat in egg yolks and gradually add the flour. Spread into prepared pan and bake for about 15 minutes. Cool slightly and spread with raspberry preserves; sprinkle with coconut.

3. Beat egg whites until stiff. Gradually beat in the remaining 1/2 cup sugar until soft peaks form. Gently fold in the pecans. Spread mixture over the raspberry preserve layer and bake again at 350 degrees for 8–10 minutes or until top is lightly golden brown. Cool and cut into 24 bars.

Per serving: 170 calories, 2 g protein, 26.5 g carbohydrate, 6.5 g fat, 3 g saturated fat, 26 mg cholesterol, .6 g fiber, 56 mg sodium. Calories from fat: 35 percent.

Apple Crisp

You can make lots of variations with this recipe. For example, instead of apples, you can use 6 cups peach slices and 2 cups raspberries for a colorful, tasty crisp.

Makes 9 servings.

- 6–8 cups sliced apples, peeled or unpeeled depending on your preference.
- 3/4 cup flour.
- 3/4 cup old-fashioned oats.
- 3/4 cup packed dark brown sugar.
- 1/2 tsp. salt.
- 3/4 tsp. ground cinnamon.
- 1/4 tsp. allspice.
- 4 tbs. butter or margarine, melted.
- 1 tsp. vanilla.
- 2 tbs. buttermilk (regular milk can also be used).

1. Preheat oven to 375 degrees. Coat 9-x9-inch baking dish with canola cooking spray. Place apple slices into prepared dish.

2. In medium bowl, blend dry ingredients. In 1 cup measure, blend butter, vanilla, and buttermilk together with fork. Drizzle butter mixture over the top of the dry ingredients and blend mixture with fork until the mixture is crumbly.

3. Sprinkle crumb mixture evenly over the fruit. Bake for 30–35 minutes or until apples are tender and top is lightly browned. Serve warm with light vanilla ice cream if desired.

Per serving: 206 calories, 2.5 g protein, 37.5 g carbohydrate, 6 g fat, 3.3 g saturated fat, 14 mg cholesterol, 2.7 g fiber, 14 mg cholesterol, 179 mg sodium. Calories from fat: 25 percent.

Chapter 7

Restaurant Rules

Dead man walking. Is that how you feel when you walk out of a restaurant after having enjoyed a rich, full meal late in the evening? It's hard to enjoy the moment of pure satisfaction after a wonderful meal when you know you are about to start paying (*big time*) for your dining indulgences—and I don't mean with your credit card. For many people, the heartburn starts to hit minutes after finishing their meal. Or, it could end up keeping you up all night.

Dine Smart

If you want to eat out in restaurants without suffering the consequences later (with acid reflux), follow these five keys toward heartburn-free dining (many of which help incorporate the 10 Food Steps to Freedom from Chapter 3).

Key 1: Select the right restaurant

Make sure you go to a restaurant that offers some acid reflux–friendly entrées or is at least willing to prepare an entrée per your special request. For example, if you have particular trouble with spices, a Thai restaurant may not be the best place for you. Or, if tomato, garlic, and onions get your goat going faster than anything, an Italian restaurant could be quite a challenge.

Key 2: Select the right menu item(s)

This sounds simple doesn't it? It's not. Here are just a few questions to ask your waiter. Remember it never hurts to ask. The only thing you stand to lose is some extra fat and calories.

- Is this dish deep-fried?
- How is this dish prepared?
- Is there any butter or oil added?
- Is this made with mayonnaise?
- Is this made with cream?
- Can this be steamed, grilled, or broiled instead of fried?

 More Americans are eating out than ever before!

In a government survey, 57 percent of Americans ate at least one food away from home on any given day in 1994–1995. In 1977–1978, this number was only 43 percent.

(*Continuing Survey of Food Intakes by Individuals or CSFII*)

- Can I have the sauce/dressing on the side?
- Can this be cooked in wine or broth instead of butter or oil?
- Can this dish be broiled or baked instead of fried?
- Can you remove the skin from my chicken before it's prepared?
- Can I substitute a salad, baked potato, or steamed vegetables for the french fries?

 What do we eat when we go out?

The number-one choice for beverages is carbonated soft drinks, followed by coffee, then milk. Favorite foods for breakfasts eaten out include eggs, toast, pancakes, sausage, or bacon. The most popular vegetable items eaten away from home are lettuce salads, french fries, mashed potatoes, and coleslaw. And as far as main entrées go, pizza and pasta items such as spaghetti come up as popular items. (The 1994 and 1995 Continuing Survey of Food Intakes by Individuals or CSFII)

Lower-fat and better-tolerated recipes for many of these favorite foods are featured in Chapter 6.

We generally eat more calories and fat when we eat out—simple as that. Studies show this again and again. Which makes sense because foods selected and eaten away from home have been reported as being higher in fat and cholesterol. But it isn't totally necessary to throw the baby away with the bathwater. It's all about choices. What do you order when you eat out?

- Can you make this dish without _____?
  (Insert whatever ingredient tends to aggravate
  your acid reflux, such as onion, garlic, or tomato.)

It goes without saying that you should order menu items that don't include the food ingredients that, without fail, help your heartburn along. If tomato products are a problem—don't go with the marinara or veal parmesan. If onions and spices spell t-r-o-u-b-l-e, then you might want to skip the 3-alarm chili. If you don't tolerate deep-fried foods well, order the grilled shrimp instead of the breaded and fried type. You get the picture.

Key 3: Select the right amount of food

Remember sometimes it isn't as much "what" you eat, as much as "how much" you eat that can send you into heartburn overdrive. Granted, eating a smaller-sized meal is a real challenge when you are eating out—especially if you are in a "celebration mode." Because what do we do when we eat out? We eat foods we don't normally eat. We eat several side dishes or courses (soup, salad, and appetizers) before we even get to the entrée we've ordered. And we enjoy our food, usually not stopping until we are filled to the brim (marked only

---

 The *no-smoking* section please!

Request the no-smoking section in restaurants to ensure your comfort while dining. Remember that cigarette smoke increases the irritation to the esophagus as you breathe it in and out.

by needing to unfasten the top button on our pants). This will probably be the toughest key to follow. But the payoff is big.

Key 4: Eat early in the evening

For so many people with acid reflux, eating late in the evening is their biggest trigger with nighttime heartburn. Say your reservation is at 7 P.M., by the time you sit down, order your dinner, and finish up the meal, it could be 9 at night by the time you pay the check! Give yourself the requisite 3–4 hours before you lie down and you won't be sawing logs until one in the morning. So count back from when you want to go to bed and you may need to make that a 5:30 or 6 P.M. dinner reservation. Look on the bright side—you'll be able to get all those early bird prices on your favorite menu items.

Key 5: Chew on it a while, would you?

A little bit of gum chewing after a meal can go a long way with heartburn prevention. Keep a pack of gum in your purse or briefcase (or car as the case may be) and you might want to top off those restaurant meals with a big stick of gum—instead of a big cup of coffee or a plate of dessert. (For more on gum chewing being a heartburn helper, see page 48.)

5 rules for low-fat food in the "fast" lane

You've been driving for hours and now, quite possibly, you are in the middle of nowhere. Your stomach has been growling at you for miles, so you decide to get off at the next exit that has a fast food chain you recognize. That's one of the best things about fast-food chains—reliability. You know what to expect whether it's a McDonald's in Nebraska or London.

Or, let's say you are running errands on your lunch hour, of which you only have 15 minutes left until you need to be back at the office. Where else can you pick up a meal in 10 minutes or less? If there is a drive-through window, you don't even have to leave your car if you don't want to. That's the other great thing about fast food—it really is fast! (The other thing about fast food is it's cheap—where else can you get lunch for $3 or less!)

Finding fast food isn't the problem when you have acid reflux—it's what to say when the person behind the window says, "Can I take your order?"

The biggest challenge for acid reflux sufferers eating at fast-food chains is probably going to be avoiding high fat foods. Over 12 years ago in my book on eating a low-fat diet without changing your lifestyle, I came up with "5 Rules for Feeding in the Fast Lane." And you now what, they still work.

Rule #1: Learn to limit total fat

Start off by ordering a sandwich or entrée with close to or less than 35 percent calories from fat. You are more likely to reach this mark if you:

F.Y.I. For your information

One-third of the people who ate out in 1994 and 1995 chose to eat at a fast-food chain (which includes pizza parlors), according to a recent government survey. *(Continuing Survey of Food Intakes by Individuals or CSFII)*

- Go for the grilled chicken sandwiches instead of the fried.
- Avoid the "deluxe," "ultimate," or "double" burgers and sandwiches.
- Follow rule #3 and #4 and cut the cream and add your own salad dressing.
- Downsize instead of "supersizing" your order of french fries and other side dishes.
- Order the smallest hamburgers instead of the bigger kind—these have more bun per burger and tend to come with ketchup and mustard instead of mayonnaise and "special sauce."

Rule #2: BYOP . . . bring your own produce

Look at any standard fast-food meal and think about the three calorie elements: fat, protein, and carbohydrate . . . and the major food categories (dairy, breads, fruits, vegetables, etc.) then ask yourself, "What's missing?" Sooner or later you'll arrive at the obvious. Most fast-food meals are sorely lacking in fruits and vegetables.

If you're lucky, some chains sell orange juice or let you make your own vegetable-packed salad. If not, you should plan to bring your own. "Bring vegetables and fruits with me?" you ask. I know this might take some getting used to. But it gets easier. I've found it's even contagious. Once you start doing this, you might find other coworkers and family members catching on, too.

Fruits and vegetables (unless they are citrus fruits or tomatoes) generally don't cause trouble for people with acid reflux and if your meal contains them, you are less likely to load up on the other high-calorie, high-fat, fast food meal items that could lead to trouble. So this point is worth practicing.

Practice #1

You just ordered the chicken breast sandwich from Wendy's along with a salad (using 2 tablespoons reduced-calorie dressing). In this case, you are only missing your fruit. You can either bring a piece of fruit with you (banana, apple, peach, etc.) or buy a bottle of 100 percent juice or a piece of fruit at the market on the way, or bring it from home.

Practice #2

You've been sitting in traffic for hours. You are tired, frustrated, and starving. Just then you spot a Taco Bell in the distance. You decide to order the bean or combo burrito containing a bread/starch, some meat or beans. But where's the fruit and vegetables? Looks like some carrot sticks and apple wedges are in order.

And remember to order your pizza with vegetables on top (skip the greasy pepperoni, salami, and sausage topping).

Rule #3: Dress your salad yourself

You may need to come equipped with some toppings. If the fast-food chain you patronize doesn't offer a low-calorie salad dressing, you still have these options:

- You can measure a couple of tablespoons of your own reduced-calorie dressing from home into a small container and bring it with you.
- If you typically munch your fast-food meal back at work, bring a bottle of your dressing to the office and keep it in the refrigerator.

Rule #4: Cut the cream (and opt for other condiments)

Many of these fast-food sandwiches come with mayonnaise, and mayonnaise-laced sauces like "special sauce" or tartar sauce. These sauces can send your sandwich into calorie and fat overload quicker than you can say, "hold the mayo." Just try squirting a little BBQ sauce, ketchup, or mustard on your sandwich instead. You can cut the fat grams in half just by having your Filet O' Fish without the tartar sauce.

Don't be afraid to order your sandwich without the mayo or special sauce. Or simply wipe it off the bun when you get it to your table.

What I like to do is tell them to add another condiment to the sandwich instead of the mayo. This seems to make them feel better—it's almost like they have to put something on the bun. So when I'm at the Wendy's drive through, I order the chicken breast filet sandwich with ketchup, lettuce, and tomato instead of mayonnaise, lettuce, and tomato.

Rule #5: Once is enough!

When I was a kid we used to go to fast food when it was someone's birthday or something equally special. Today, people go on an almost daily basis. It's survival in this fast-paced life we all lead.

How much fast food is too much? It really depends on each individual. For my family, we try to go no more than once a week. This isn't necessarily because fast food is so "bad" for us (we all make healthier choices when we go to fast food), it's just that homemade food—eaten in a relaxed family environment—is so much "better."

If you put convenience first (maybe even cost) you might be driving through those golden arches almost every day. Not only does that encourage a total diet that is low in fruits, vegetables, fiber, and phytochemicals and rich in extra calories, fat, and sugar, but it makes fast food so standard, that it isn't special anymore.

What else should you know about fast food?

Besides the whole high-fat food thing, there are a few other things about fast-food dining that can greatly challenge your desire to be heartburn-free.

- It's "fast food" after all, right? So guess what, we tend to eat our food—fast. Eating slowly will help the food go down in relaxed manner. If we eat our meal slowly we may also avoid overeating. You have to give your stomach time to register to your brain that it's filling up. If you literally shovel it down in 5 minutes or less, you never give your tummy time to check in with your brain.

- How are you going to wet your whistle? Your beverage choices in fast-food chains are limited to soda, coffee, and milk. The only other beverage I've seen offered is orange juice and this high-acid drink may not be the best thing if you have acid reflux (it can bother some people). The calcium in milk can stimulate the stomach to release acid, so this may not work either. It is possible to order ice water—all you have to do is ask for it. I do it all the time.

- Everything about fast food is about more, more, more. Supersize this, meal deal that. Eating fast food is definitely going to test your desire to eat small-sized meals (and avoid eating big). I know this is cheating, but if I want a hamburger, I order the kid's meal hamburger. I get a nice, small hamburger (that automatically comes with ketchup and mustard and not mayonnaise) and I get a few bites of fries (which is all I really want) and a drink. And even if I'm feeling like a chocolate shake, most of the chains will make you a kid-size shake instead. Again, this is just enough milkshake to satisfy me. And I get a toy, too! (I haven't quite outgrown that part.)

On the road is the worst!

When you have acid reflux and you are traveling for business or pleasure, this has got to be one of your most difficult times. All the acid reflux red flags are up and waving in your face.

You don't sleep well when you are traveling to begin with. Then your bed is flat and you don't have your special, extra fluffy pillow.

You are eating food you don't normally eat for starters. And you are eating out breakfast, lunch, and dinner, making it triple hard to follow the 10 Food Steps to Freedom.

Unless you want to eat alone, you have no choice but to follow the work crowd and eat those darn late dinners. When you are traveling on business, most of the dinner meetings are "late" dinner meetings. Then everyone hits the sack when they get back to the hotel room so they can be bright-eyed and bushy-tailed for the morning meetings.

Usually travel is stressful. Plane delays throw your eating and your comfort level off schedule. You wait in lines for everything. Then once you get there you are "on duty," answering questions about your project or products, meeting new clients, etc. Any way you slice it, it's stressful.

So what can you do? Try your hardest to follow the 10 Food Steps to Freedom—especially now that you are traveling. And always carry some trusty medications with you, just in case.

Glossary

abdominal Pertaining to the abdomen, the part of the body between the thorax and the pelvis.

alkaline Basic; the opposite of acidic.

calorie The amount of energy or heat needed to raise the temperature of one gram of water one degree Celsius.

carbohydrate One of the three main types of nutrition, consisting primarily of sugars and starches; provides a ready source of energy to the body.

cholesterol Functions as a precursor molecule in various metabolic pathways but in too much quantity may cause arteriosclerosis.

chronic Having a long duration or frequent recurrences.

diagnosis The identification of a disease from its symptoms.

esophagus The muscular tube down which food travels from the back of the throat to the stomach.

fiber Mostly indigestible material in food that stimulates the intestine to peristalsis.

laryngitis An inflammation of the larynx, the passageway through which air passes to the lungs.

metabolize To process a substance, such as food; to turn food into energy.

neutralize To counteract the effects of; specifically, the effect of adding a base to an acid is to neutralize the acid.

overindulge To have too much of something.

prevention The process of keeping something, such as a disease, from occurring.

protein One of the three main types of nutrition. Made up of amino acids, proteins include many essential biological compounds (such as enzymes, hormones, and antibodies).

secrete To release some material that performs a specific useful function, such as saliva or mucous.

side effect A secondary—usually negative—effect of something, such as a drug.

susceptible Vulnerable or prone.

symptom A physical sensation—usually uncomfortable—caused by a disease.

ulcer A break in the skin or lining; a gastric ulcer is situated in the stomach.

For More Information

American College of Gastroenterology
P.O. Box 342260
Bethesda, MD 20827-2260
(301) 263-9000
Web site: http://www.acg.gi.org
The goal of the American College of Gastroenterology
(ACG) is "to advance the scientific study and medical
practice of diseases of the gastrointestinal (GI) tract." The
organization provides resources for both patients and
physicians.

North American Society for Pediatric
    Gastroenterology, Hepatology, and Nutrition
    (NASPGHAN)
P.O. Box 6
Flourtown, PA 19031
(215) 233-0808
Web site: http://www.naspghan.org
According to its Web site, "The mission of the North
American Society for Pediatric Gastroenterology,
Hepatology, and Nutrition is to be a world leader in
advancing the science and clinical practice of Pediatric
Gastroenterology, Hepatology and Nutrition in health and
disease."

The National Institute of Diabetes and Digestive and Kidney Diseases (NIDDK)
Office of Communications & Public Liaison
NIDDK, NIH
Building 31, Rm 9A06
31 Center Drive, MSC 2560
Bethesda, MD 20892-2560
(301) 496-3583
Part of the National Institutes of Health (NIH) and the U.S. Department of Health and Human Services, the National Institute of Diabetes and Digestive and Kidney Diseases (NIDDK) conducts and supports research on many diseases, including acid reflux and other digestive issues.

Web Sites
Due to the changing nature of Internet links, Rosen Publishing has developed an online list of Web sites related to the subject of this book. This site is updated regularly. Please use this link to access the list:

http://www.rosenlinks.com/tmwe/acre

For Further Reading

Cass, Hyla. *Supplement Your Prescription: What Your Doctor Doesn't Know About Nutrition*. Laguna Beach, CA: Basic Health Pub., 2007.

Challa, Shekhar Kumar, M.D. *Spurn the Burn: Treat the Heat; Everything You Need to Know to Beat Acid Reflux Disease*. Topeka, KS: Kansas Medical Pub., 2005.

FC&A Medical Publishing, eds. *The Complete Guide to Digestive Health: Plain Answers About IBS, Constipation, Diarrhea, Heartburn, Ulcers, and More*. Peachtree City, GA: FC&A Medical Pub., 2006.

Hinder, Ronald A., ed. *Gastroesophageal Reflux Disease*. Austin, TX: R. G. Landes, 1993.

Minocha, Anil, and Christine Adamec. *How to Stop Heartburn: Simple Ways to Heal Heartburn and Acid Reflux*. New York, NY: Wiley, 2001.

Miskovitz, Paul F., and Marian Betancourt. *The Doctor's Guide to Gastrointestinal Health: Preventing and Treating Acid Reflux, Ulcers, Irritable Bowel Syndrome, Diverticulitis, Celiac Disease, Colon Cancer, Pancreatitis, Cirrhosis, Hernias and More*. Hoboken, NJ: Wiley, 2005.

Rubin, Jordan, and Joseph Brasco. *The Great Physician's Rx for Heartburn and Acid Reflux*. Nashville, TN: Thomas Nelson, 2007.

Scarpignato, C., ed. *Advances in Drug Therapy of Gastroesophageal Reflux Disease*. New York, NY: Karger, 1992.

Shimberg, Elaine Fantle. *Coping with Chronic Heartburn: What You Need to Know About Acid Reflux and GERD*. New York, NY: St. Martin's Press, 2001.

Sklar, Jill. *Eating for Acid Reflux: A Handbook and Cookbook for Those with Heartburn*. New York, NY: Marlowe, 2003.

Index

About the Author

Elaine Magee, M.P.H., R.D., is the author of the celebrated syndicated column "The Recipe Doctor." Elaine is a regular contributor to *Parenting* and *Woman's Day* and is the author of eighteen books on nutrition and cooking, including *The Recipe Doctor* as well as the previous books in the *Tell Me What to Eat* series. She has her own Web site (recipedoctor.com) and contributes to several Web sites, including dietriot.com.